HOW TO TAKE CARE OF YOUR HEART

In this Series

other titles in preparation

How To Books: General Editor Roland Seymour

TAKE CARE OF YOUR HEART

DR MARK PAYNE
MA (Oxon) MB BS (London) MRCS LRCP (London)

Northcote House

DEDICATION
To Lynn

First published in 1989 by Northcote House Publishers Ltd, Harper & Row House, Estover Road, Plymouth PL6 7PZ, United Kingdom. Tel: Plymouth (0752) 705251. Telex: 45635. Fax: (0752) 777603.

British Library Cataloguing in Publication Data

Payne, Mark, *1952-*
  How to take care of your heart
  1. Man. Heart. Coronary diseases. Prevention
  I. Title
  616.1'2305

  ISBN 0-7463-0563-X

Typeset by Cheshire Typesetters
Printed in Great Britain by BPCC Wheatons Ltd, Exeter

Contents

Foreword

Dr Mark Payne is well known for his innovative approach to the provision of family doctor medicine. His medical qualifications are rooted in the Oxford academic world — a factor which will no doubt be readily appreciated by the reflection of his humour in the cartoons reproduced in this book.

At the time of writing the Government's implementation of proposals made in a White Paper entitled *Promoting Better Health: The Government's Programme for Improving Primary Health Care* is still awaited. However, it was clear from this document that one of the key issues to be addressed is how to promote health and prevent illness within the general population. Whilst it is acknowledged that there has been good progress in the prevention and control of disease through many public health initiatives, there remains the difficulty of the self-inflicted illnesses — as a result of smoking, for example.

Encouraging the population to accept greater responsibility for its own good health is attractive for obvious reasons, particularly at a time when the National Health Service is being pressed to meet the ever-increasing demands that modern medical practice imposes. It was out of this thinking that the 'Oxford Project' was born several years ago. Simplicity is its greatest strength — encouraging patients to develop a healthier lifestyle. It concentrates on issues such as smoking habits, diet, weight and blood pressure monitoring. Dr Payne's contribution to this sort of approach — cheap but nevertheless effective — is admirably reflected in his latest publication.

The item on blood pressure is a good example of a refreshing approach by a medic, recognising that patients may be interested, for example, in how blood pressure is measured and to some extent judged. This may seem a relatively minor point, but I have to admit that after 25 years within health service management I was still blissfully unaware of the mysteries of blood pressure readings.

The book offers a simple message — our need to accept more responsibility for our own wellbeing. We should be indebted to Mark Payne for providing a handbook on this most important subject, which should be close to all our hearts.

Keith W. Higgins, Administrator
Solihull Family Practitioner Committee

Introduction

THE PRESENT POSITION

- Heart attacks in Britain now cause one in three deaths among people aged 55-64 years.

- Heart disease kills a greater proportion of the British population than that of almost any other nation in the world.

- Many heart attacks can be prevented by attention to the known causes, often called *risk factors*.

- The major known risk factors are cigarette smoking, high blood pressure and excess fat circulating in the blood.

- If you are unfortunate enough to suffer a heart attack, the key to survival is getting to a hospital *as soon as possible*. Of the patients who are going to die of a heart attack 50% do so within two hours of the onset of the chest pain.

- Heart attacks can be most successfully treated in the coronary care unit of a well equipped modern hospital.

THIS BOOK

This book is written for the proverbial man or woman on top of the Clapham omnibus. It has two functions:

- To tell you the symptoms of a heart attack so that you will recognise one quickly and get appropriate treatment.

- To reduce your chances of suffering a heart attack by bringing to your attention the known risk factors. These factors are discussed in detail and concrete suggestions are given explaining *how to avoid a heart attack*.

Finally, it is often not easy to be sure that someone has had a heart attack but if in doubt **always seek medical advice immediately.**

ACKNOWLEDGEMENTS

An author is a product of his genes, his environment and, most importantly, his teachers. My environment has been shaped largely by my teachers, and my interest in ideas has been stimulated by their personalities and enthusiasm. I am indebted to these people, and in particular to my parents who planted the magic seed of curiosity, and taught me how to work on a project.

The writing of this book has been made considerably easier by the enthusiastic support of Miss Donna Jackson, Mr Mike Porter and especially my family. Finally, the credit for the remarkable ability of turning hieroglyphics into a high quality manuscript must go to Mrs Margaret Shepheard.

1
How to Recognise and Survive a Heart Attack

PROFILE OF A HEART ATTACK

The patient
It may be difficult to recognise a potential heart attack victim in every case, but the likely candidate will probably have several of these characteristics:

- Male aged 50 years plus
- Female aged 60 years plus
- A cigarette smoker
- A sufferer from high blood pressure
- Overweight
- Unfit
- Stressed

The symptoms
An attack can occur unprovoked but is more likely to occur after exertion, excitement, stress or anger, or extremes of temperature.

The usual picture is:

- A central chest pain
- Shortness of breath
- Sweating
- Giddiness with nausea

NB: It is not necessary to have all these symptoms to have a heart attack.

The causes
A heart attack is caused by a **sudden blocking** of one or both of the two arteries supplying the heart muscle (see fig. 1). In 90% of cases this blockage occurs due to a fatty change called *atheroma* (Greek for

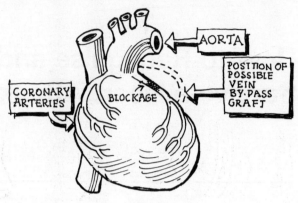

Fig. 1

'porridge') in which the wall of the artery becomes filled with a deposit of **cholesterol** (see fig. 2) and the heart muscle becomes starved of blood.

These fatty deposits usually occur within 1-1½ inches from the beginning of the coronary artery. (One of the surgical treatments for heart disease — a coronary artery by-pass operation — involves creating an alternative route around the blockage, using a vein from the leg.) There are often no symptoms until 50% of the artery is filled, and at this stage the condition of **angina** may occur with exercise, excitement/stress, temperature extremes or after a large meal or cigarette.

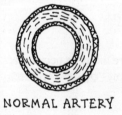

NORMAL ARTERY   ARTERY WITH ATHEROMA

Fig. 2

A heart attack occurs when there is a sudden extra blockage of one or both of the coronary arteries. The lack of blood initially causes pain, followed by death of the heart muscle if the interruption persists for longer than one hour.

PAINS THAT MAY MIMIC A HEART ATTACK

There are numerous other pains in the chest that can mimic a heart attack. Chest pain may be produced by any of the structures in the chest;

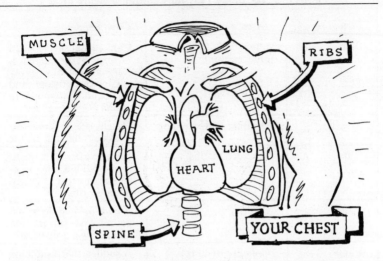

Fig. 3: Your chest

Fig. 3 shows the structures involved. Table 1 (p.14) gives details of the other sorts of chest pains that can commonly be confused with a heart attack. The table is given for information only. **Do not try to come to a diagnosis yourself. If there is a possibility of heart attack consult your doctor immediately!**

SURVIVING A HEART ATTACK

The ambulance
If it is suspected that you *are* having a heart attack you will find yourself speeding to hospital in an ambulance. Most heart patients are sat upright rather than laid flat since it makes their breathing easier. They are given oxygen through a mask, which helps the heart to beat more firmly and prevents unconsciousness.

In some cities, like Belfast and Brighton, there are special ambulances called Mobile Coronary Care Units (MCCU). These are equipped with ECG machines and resuscitation equipment which the paramedics who travel with the vehicle are trained to use.

The hospital
When you get to hospital the doctor will try and come to a precise diagnosis of the cause of your chest pain by:

● asking appropriate questions to rule out other causes of chest pain as already outlined in Table 1;

● examining you thoroughly, to look for important signs such as an

Table 1 Other pains that may mimic a heart attack

Structure	Disease causing pain	Comments
Skin	Shingles (a form of chicken pox)	Can cause severe pain *before* rash appears. Rash almost always occurs on one side only and as a band. Commoner in adults 60 years plus.
Muscle	Bruising and straining	Usually occurs within two weeks of muscular effort.
Ribs	Fracture of ribs	Usually after damage to chest wall but may occasionally occur due to diseased ribs.
Lung	Pleurisy	A sharp, well localised pain worse on moving and taking a deep breath.
Lung	Collapse of lung (pneumothorax)	A sudden sharp stabbing possibly associated with breathlessness. Commoner in tall, young men.
Lung	Blood clot (pulmonary embolus)	Often associated with a clot in calf, a recent operation or injury.
Oesophagus	Indigestion (hiatus hernia)	Worse when lying flat or bending over. Often better with antacids.
Stomach	Indigestion (peptic ulcer)	Often associated with meals. Often better with antacids.
Gall bladder	Infection/ inflammation of gall bladder (cholecystitis)	Often starts after a fatty meal. Commoner in women.
Spine	Damage to bone	A very sharp pain from the back, often worse in one position.
Large artery (aorta)	Blow-out (aneurysm)	Caused by the different layers of the aorta separating from each other.
Heart	Angina	Caused by a temporary lack of blood supply to the heart. If angina lasts longer than a quarter of an hour then suspect a heart attack.
Heart	Pericarditis	Inflammation of the membrane surrounding the heart.

Table 2 The doctor's questions	
Factor studied by doctor	*Most likely response for a heart attack*
Age	50 years plus
Sex	Male (women do have heart attacks but their hormones tend to protect them until the menopause)
Occupation	High stress job
Site of pain	Central chest pain
Nature of pain	Like a heavy weight or a tight band around the chest
Frequency of pain	Continuous
Length of pain	Greater than half an hour
Severity of pain	Usually severe (may be painless especially in old people)
Factors that make pain worse	Exertion (not reliable)
Factors that make pain better	Rest (not reliable)
Associated factors	Shortness of breath, sweating, pale, dizziness and nausea
Radiation of pain	Into left or both arms, neck and jaw
Cause of pain	Possibly unaccustomed exercise especially in the cold
General health	Often unwell for one week with recent high stress in previous three months
State of heart	Angina and previous heart disease
State of arteries	Previous strokes
State of blood pressure	Previous high blood pressure
Other diseases	Diabetes, gout, other illnesses
Medication	Insulin, contraceptive pill
Smoking habits	Smoker
Drinking habits	Heavy drinker, more than 6 units a day (see p.27)
Health of family	Family history of heart attacks, raised blood pressure and high blood fats
Exercise habits	Little or no exercise
Diet	High in animal fat

irregular pulse rate, low or high blood pressure, unexpected sounds
from the heart, congestion of the lungs and swollen ankles;

● carrying out special tests such as an electrocardiogram (ECG), chest
X-ray and blood tests for 'cardiac enzymes'.

The doctor's questions

The questions asked by the doctor are designed to prove or disprove
the likelihood of a heart attack. Typical questions are set out in Table
2 (p.15) in the left-hand column. In the right-hand column of Table
2 are answers that are more likely to be associated with a heart attack.

The doctor's examination

The doctor will have to examine your whole body in order to identify
problems with the heart. For example, ankle swelling (oedema) will suggest heart failure, and changes in the blood vessels in the back of the
eye will suggest raised blood pressure.

The electrocardiograph (ECG)

This is the quickest and usually the best test to confirm the diagnosis
of a heart attack. Sometimes, however, there is no change in the ECG
after a heart attack, or else the change may take 24 hours to develop.

The ECG is an electrical tracing of the heart muscle made by attaching
wires to the four limbs and front of the chest and is quite painless. The
ECG machine picks up tiny electric currents flowing within the heart

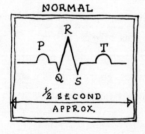
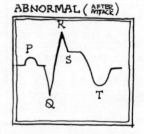

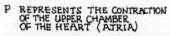
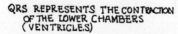

P REPRESENTS THE CONTRACTION
OF THE UPPER CHAMBER
OF THE HEART (ATRIA)

QRS REPRESENTS THE CONTRACTION
OF THE LOWER CHAMBERS
(VENTRICLES)

T REPRESENTS THE ELECTRICAL
RECOVERY OF THE VENTRICLES
BACK TO THE RESTING STATE

P WAVE IS UNCHANGED

Q WAVE IS DEEPER

ST SEGMENT IS ELEVATED

T WAVE IS INVERTED

Fig. 4: The ECG

muscle, and converts them into a tracing on a strip of graph paper (see Fig. 4 — note that the letters PQRST used to name the different parts of the wave have been chosen arbitrarily).

The ECG is an invaluable aid in the coronary care unit. It gives essential information about the heart's rate and rhythm. Abnormal rhythms can be identified and treated before they become life threatening.

Occasionally the ECG may give no help or may be difficult to interpret, in which case blood tests for cardiac enzymes are taken.

Cardiac enzymes
Substances called **cardiac enzymes** are released into the blood after a heart attack due to damage to the heart muscle fibres (see Fig. 5). (Tests for these enzymes are not necessary if the ECG confirms that a heart attack has occurred.)

The first enzyme is called **creatine phosphokinase (CPK),** and rises to its maximum level 24 hours after a heart attack. The second enzyme is called **lactic dehydrogenase (LDH),** which rises to its maximum level 48 to 72 hours after a heart attack. These tests are positive in approximately 90% of heart attacks.

The total amount of the enzyme CPK released into the blood will give a good indication of the size of the heart attack: the more heart muscle destroyed by the heart attack the more CPK released.

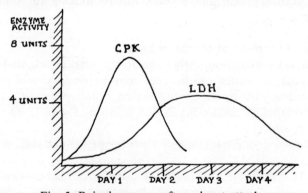

Fig. 5: Raised enzymes after a heart attack

Management of the patient
This should take place in a hospital coronary care unit (or intensive care unit), with facilities for 24-hour ECG monitoring, and rapid resuscitation if necessary in the event of a cardiac arrest.

Once the heart attack has been confirmed, the patient is put on strict bed rest, and pain relief will be given if necessary by an injection of morphine or a similar drug. There is little or no chance of addiction, since the morphine is required only to counteract pain. Oxygen is sometimes given continously via a mask in the acute stages if there are complications.

A relatively new development in the treatment of heart attacks is the use of 'clotbusters' (streptokinase and tissue plasminogen activator). These drugs are capable of dissolving the clot blocking the coronary artery. If these clotbusters are injected into a vein within six hours of the onset of the chest pain, the chance of death from a heart attack is almost halved. In the future it is quite likely that they will be administered by the general practitioner or ambulance crew before a heart attack patient is taken to hospital.

In addition, on some occasions, anticoagulants (such as heparin or warfarin) may be given to reduce the risk of clots or emboli being formed.

The main complications are dealt with in the next section. Details of resuscitation are covered in Chapter 13.

COMMON ACUTE COMPLICATIONS
(within first week)

Most complications arise due to damage to the heart's electrical conducting system rather than due to the destruction of heart muscle fibres. In the coronary care unit doctors will be looking for four main problems.

Abnormal rhythms of the heart beat
These tend to occur at an early stage after a heart attack, and are the main cause of sudden death. They may be detected and precisely diagnosed only the by the use of the electrocardiogram (ECG), hence the importance of continuous ECG monitoring for 48-72 hours after the heart attack.

Abnormal rhythms are treated either by the use of drugs, or by the use of an electric DC shock (cardio version) given by a defibrillator, or, if the heart beats too slowly, by using a 'cardiac pacemaker'.

Low blood pressure
This may occur due to irregular or unsatisfactory heart beats, damage to heart muscle or valves, or due to drugs given for pain relief at the time of the heart attack. If low blood pressure persists, it indicates severe damage to the heart muscle, and so poor chances of survival of the patient.

Cardiac failure
This is related to low blood pressure, and is a partial failure of the heart to pump an adequate supply of blood around the body. Blood tends to accumulate either in the lowest parts of the body, giving ankle swelling (right ventricular failure), or else in the lungs, giving breathlessness (left ventricular failure).

Clots (thromboses and emboli)
A thrombosis in the calf muscle of the leg or else on the heart muscle at the site of the heart attack may occur. This clot may dislodge itself and float around in the blood stream (an embolus), eventually coming to rest in the lungs or brain respectively.

QUESTIONS TO ASK THE DOCTOR

When you have a relative in hospital with a heart attack you may find the situation intimidating and be reluctant to ask about the patient's progress. Here are some useful questions that you could ask the doctor or ward sister:

● What is the exact diagnosis? (Don't be afraid to ask for an explanation in simple non-technical terms.)

● How is the patient progressing? Are there any problems at present?

● What are the likely complications and when might they occur?

● Can I do anything to help?

DISCHARGE FROM HOSPITAL

After seven to fourteen days in hospital, if there are no complications, the patient may be discharged home. In order to return to fitness, a gentle exercise programme should begin. A reasonable target would be to walk approximately one mile a day one month after the heart attack. The patient should try to reduce all risk factors (see Chapter 2) and take all medication as prescribed.

Car driving is not advisable for two to three months, and it is wise to have a check-up with a GP before starting to drive again. (Unfortunately, however, HGV and PSV drivers and airline pilots are forbidden to drive or fly their machines again because of the possible disastrous consequences of another heart attack.)

SUMMARY

- Heart attacks are very common.

- A heart attack patient will usually have one or more of the following characteristics: male over 50 years or female over 60 years, cigarette smoker, high blood pressure, overweight, unfit, stressed.

- The typical picture includes central chest pain, shortness of breath, sweating with giddiness and nausea.

- A heart attack may occur without chest pain, especially in older patients.

- Survival depends on early diagnosis and getting to hospital quickly.

- Heart attacks are life threatening. **If there is a possibility that a heart attack has occurred consult a doctor immediately.**

2
The Risk Factors for
a Heart Attack

THE SIZE OF THE PROBLEM

Prior to the 1930s heart attacks were relatively rare. Now they occur in epidemic proportions. In Britain there are 300,000 heart attacks per year and 180,000 patients per year die of heart attacks, and almost half the premature deaths in men (aged 45 to 65) are due to this cause.

To put these figures in a more graphic perspective, the deaths from heart attacks in Britain are equivalent to a fully laden 500 seater jumbo jet crashing without survivors *every single day of the year*.

This is particularly staggering when you realise that the yearly deaths from cancer of the lung are 40,000, and from road traffic accidents and suicides a far lower figure of 5,000 each.

Encouraging news

In 1981 the Royal College of General Practitioners stated, 'About a quarter of all deaths from coronary artery disease (heart attacks) in people under 70 are probably preventable by the application of existing medical knowledge.' Put in another way, heart attacks may be prevented by attention to the risk factors that make a heart attack more likely to occur in an individual.

The risk factors

There are three main risk factors for heart attacks:

- Cigarette smoking
- High blood pressure
- Excess fat in the blood.

And there are other risk factors of variable importance:

- Obesity
- Diabetes
- Lack of exercise
- Family tendency to heart attacks
- Stress
- Personality type
- Alcohol
- Oral contraceptive pill
- Gout
- Soft water.

By studying these risk factors it is possible to single out people who have a high risk of suffering a heart attack in the next five years. If they can reduce as much as possible the amount of each risk factor, they will then lower the overall risk, and almost certainly improve their health and increase their life expectancy.

You will be able to calculate your own risk of a heart attack by using the chart given in Chapter 3. The following chapters then give you plenty of ideas and suggestions of how to reduce the level of each risk factor.

THE MAJOR RISK FACTORS

The major risk factors are not independent of one another, but rather interact, and if you have two major risk factors the heart risk is considerably greater than if you have just one. So it follows that having all three major risk factors is even worse.

The cumulative risk can be expressed in the following table.

Number of major risk factors	Heart attack risk
0	x 1
1	x 2
2	x 4
3	x 9

In addition, if there is any existing blockage of the heart arteries or history of a previous heart attack, the likelihood of a further heart attack is also greatly increased.

Cigarette smoking

This is **the most important cause** of heart attacks, and the single most helpful thing that you can do to reduce your risk is to **stop smoking.** Each year about 40,000 men and women under 65 die from heart attacks and 25% of these deaths are believed to be caused by cigarette smoking.

The risk is particularly great for men under 45 smoking more than 25 cigarettes a day. Such men are 10-15 times more likely to die than non-smokers.

Women smokers are also more likely to die at an early age, especially if they have taken the oral contraceptive; however, their risk is still less than that for men.

The two most important constituents of tobacco smoke causing damage to the heart are **nicotine** and **carbon monoxide.** The amount absorbed depends on the number of cigarettes smoked and whether or not the smoke is inhaled.

The effects of cigarette smoking include:

- Making the heart beat faster, and raising the blood pressure. These two changes have the effect of making the heart work harder and increasing its need for oxygen.
- The release of adrenalin and similar substances which tend to make the heart beat irregularly.
- Reducing the oxygen carrying capacity of the blood. This is caused by carbon monoxide which is present in cigarette smoke at a level about 8 times greater than the maximum permitted in industry.
- Damage to the lining of the coronary artery caused by carbon monoxide.
- Increasing the stickiness of platelets in the blood, encouraging clots and thromboses.
- Increasing the level of a protein in the blood called **fibrinogen** which encourages clotting. It has been suggested that the level of

SMOKING

fibrinogen in the blood is, on its own, a good predictor of the likelihood of sustaining a heart attack.

● Changing the nature of the fat in the blood.

High blood pressure

There is a well established direct link between raised blood pressure and heart attacks. High blood pressure is exceptionally common, affecting approximately 20% of the population in Britain, and in 90% to 95% of these cases no cause can be found for the problem. Whenever blood pressure is measured two figures are given, for example:

$$\frac{120}{80} = \frac{\text{systolic pressure of 120mm of mercury}}{\text{diastolic pressure of 80mm of mercury}}$$

The upper figure (120) is called the **systolic blood pressure** and the lower figure (80) is called the **diastolic blood pressure.** These are the maximum and minimum pressures respectively of the blood within the main arteries, and are given in units of millimetres of mercury. The World Health Organisation has defined the upper limits of normal blood pressure as 160/95 (see Chapter 6).

Both the systolic and diastolic blood pressures are important in determining the risk of heart attacks, but blood pressure varies enormously from day to day, and even from one part of a day to another in the same individual. Also, in general, as you get older your blood pressure goes up. It is usual to take several readings, at intervals of several weeks, before high blood pressure is diagnosed.

To find out your blood pressure ask your local GP to measure it for you.

Excess blood fats

It is only in recent years that the full significance of this major risk factor has been appreciated. Blood fats consist of two components, **cholesterol** and **triglyceride,** either of which, if raised, may cause a heart attack.

The more important blood fat is cholesterol, and there is a large variation in average blood levels from country to country. In Japan, for instance, where a typical cholesterol level is 4.5 mmol/l (a unit of concentration), heart attacks are rare, whereas in Britain, where a typical level is 5.9 mmol/l, heart attacks are very common.

Blood fat levels are raised by a diet containing a lot of animal fats (saturated) which are solid at room temperature. Blood fat levels are reduced by a diet containing a moderate amount of vegetable oils (unsaturated) which are liquid at room temperature, while fish oils — especially from herring, mackerel, salmon, sardines and tuna — containing eicosapentaenoic acid (EPA) may actually even protect against the risk of a heart attack by lowering the blood triglyceride level.

To find out whether your blood cholesterol level is raised ask your GP to arrange a blood test, for which there should be no charge

OTHER RISK FACTORS

Obesity
Being overweight tends to cause a rise in the level of blood fats, blood

pressure and blood sugar. It also means a reduction in the amount of exercise taken. All these factors increase the likelihood of a heart attack.

Diabetes
Diabetes greatly increases the risk of a heart attack, especially in women. Heart attacks cause 50% of all deaths in diabetics.

Diabetes is caused by a complete or partial lack of the hormone **insulin,** produced from the pancreas. A severe form of diabetes occurs in young people, but a more common and less severe type is associated with obesity and occurs in adults over 50 years.

Lack of exercise
Vigorous exercise appears to reduce the risk of a heart attack. However, obese people rarely exert themselves vigorously enough and exercise also does not protect them against heart attacks in the presence of other strong risk factors, such as heavy smoking. Regular physical exercise does, however, reduce the tendency of the blood to clot, and improves the fitness of the heart muscle.

Family tendency

Sometimes heart attacks seem to run in families. The problem is usually explained by an inherited tendency towards raised blood levels of fat (hyperlipidaemia) or high blood pressure.

HEREDITY

If one or more members of the family sustain a heart attack before age 55, it is very important that the other members of the family are screened to exclude raised blood fats. This disease of raised blood fats occurs in approximately 1 in 300 of the general population, but if one member of the family has it then other members are very likely to suffer from it as well.

If this hereditary problem is found early and quickly treated premature death can be avoided in most cases.

Stress

Certain occupations are considered as high stress jobs, eg salesmen, and they are associated with an increasing risk of heart attacks. Stress, excitement or anger, in the short term, have each been shown to precipitate angina or heart attacks, and in the long term, too many stressful events in one year can foreshadow a heart attack.

Personality type

American research suggests that there are basically two personality types (see Chapter 9). Type A personalities (ambitious perfectionists) are more liable to heart attacks than type B (placid non-achievers). This view is less popular in the UK. The important factor may be not so much the ambition, but whether or not the individual is successful (fulfilment and thus low stress) or unsuccessful (frustration and thus high stress) in his or her endeavours.

Excessive alcohol intake

Excessive alcohol intake is associated with cigarette smoking, raised blood pressure and raised blood fats, as well as many other lesser risk factors. Not surprisingly, people with a high alcohol intake are more likely to suffer a heart attack.

Alcohol consumption deserves special attention because reducing intake to one to two units a day (one unit = half a pint normal strength beer or lager, one glass of sherry/wine or one measure of spirits) can eliminate drinking as a risk factor.

THE PILL

The contraceptive pill

There is evidence to suggest that the contraceptive pill damages arteries and thus causes an increased risk of a heart attack, especially if the pill has been taken for five years or more. The risk is greater in women over 35, especially if they have other risk factors such as smoking, raised blood pressure, raised blood fats or diabetes.

Gout

Heart attacks are more common in gout sufferers, 95% of whom are men. It is not clear whether it is the gout that causes the heart attacks, or whether it is merely associated with high blood pressure, obesity, raised blood fats and increased clotting of the platelets.

Soft water

Studies around the world have linked heart attacks with soft water. The reason for this link is unknown.

GOUT

SUMMARY

- Heart attacks may be prevented by attention to the risk factors.

- The three main risk factors for heart attacks are cigarette smoking, high blood pressure and excess fats in the blood.

- Other risk factors include obesity, diabetes, lack of exercise, family tendency to heart attacks, stress, personality type, the contraceptive pill, excessive alcohol intake, gout and soft water.

3
How to Calculate Your Own Risk of a Heart Attack

The previous chapter listed the risk factors that may cause a heart attack. This chapter enables you to calculate your own risk of suffering a heart attack. It is based on the Framingham Study, carried out in the town of Framingham, Massachusetts, USA. The study has been going on for 40 years and was started to try to find the causes of heart attacks in America. It involves the regular examination of all adults living in the town and has provided a lot of the initial evidence about risk factors for heart attacks. I am grateful to Dr William P. Castelli MD, Medical Director of the study, for permission to use the cardiovascular risk score method which appears on the next page.

RISK CALCULATION

The chart on p.30 is provided so that you can calculate your own risk. You will have to know the following factors in order to complete the chart:

- Your blood pressure (systolic and diastolic pressure). You may find this out from your NHS general practitioner.
- Number of cigarettes smoked per day.
- The number of your close relatives (mother, father, sister, brother, son and daughter) suffering from angina or heart attacks before the age of 55 years.
- Your serum cholesterol level. Your local NHS general practitioner should be able to arrange for you to have this measured without charge.
- Your weight in kilograms. (There is a conversion table in the appendix to convert from stones and pounds to kilograms.)
- Your height in centimetres. (There is a conversion table in the appendix to convert from feet and inches to centimetres.)

Cardiovascular Risk Score				
Factor	Score	Number of points scored on	Number of points scored on	Number of points scored on ....
Male	1			
Female	0			
Systolic blood pressure in mm mercury:				
Greater than 200	4			
161-200	2			
140-160	1			
Less than 140	0			
Diastolic blood pressure in mm mercury:				
Greater than 120	4			
111-120	2			
90-110	1			
Less than 90	0			
Number of cigarettes smoked per day:				
Greater than 40	7			
21-40	5			
11-20	3			
1-10	1			
0	0			
Family history of heart disease (mother, father, sister, brother, son, daughter with angina or heart attacks aged younger than 55):				
5 relatives	10			
4 relatives	8			
3 relatives	6			
2 relatives	4			
1 relative	2			
0 relatives	0			
Cholesterol (mmol/l):				
Greater than 9	8			
7.0-9.0	6			
5.5-7.0	4			
4.5-5.5	2			
Less than 4.5	0			
Body Mass Index (Quetelet Index) $= \dfrac{Wt(kg) \times 1000}{[Ht\ (cm)]^2}$				
Greater than 2.75	2			
Less than 2.75	0			
Total:				

● You will need a calculator to work out the Quetelet Index of Body Mass which is equal to the weight in kilograms x 1,000 over the height in centimetres squared:

$$\frac{(\text{Weight in kilograms x 1,000})}{(\text{Height in centimetres})^2}$$

The Body Mass Index tells you whether you are overweight for your height and whether you are likely to have any health consequences.

Body Mass Index

Less than 2.0 Underweight with health consequences
2.0   -   2.5 Acceptable weight
2.5   -   3.0 Mild obesity
More than 3.0 Moderate obesity with health consequences
More than 4.0 Severe obesity with severe health consequences

The points in each category are added together to give your total score. This total score is then compared against the Risk Index given below.

Cardiovascular Risk Index

Low Risk	0- 5 points
Moderate Risk	6- 9 points
Elevated Risk	10-15 points
High Risk	16 plus points

If you find that your score is moderate, elevated or high then you should read the following chapters, paying attention to the instructions in the summary. Act upon these instructions, and recalculate your risk in 3-6 months time to see if it has dropped, then check your score every year to ensure that it has not crept up.

Worked example 1

Mr Smith, blood pressure 210/115, smokes 30 cigarettes a day. He has two close relatives with angina and another who has had a heart attack, all under 55 years of age. His blood cholesterol level is 7.3 mmol/l, his height is 5'6" and his weight is 14st 3lb.

$$\text{Calculation of Quetelet Index} = \frac{\text{Wt (kg) x 1,000}}{[\text{Ht (cm)}]^2}$$

$$\text{Weight 14st 3lb} = 90.3 \text{ kg}$$

$$\text{Height 5'6"} = 167 \text{ cm}$$

$$\text{Quetelet Index} = \frac{90.3 \times 1,000}{(167)^2}$$

$$= \frac{90,300}{28,889}$$

$$= 3.237$$

Thus Mr Smith's Quetelet Index is greater than 2.75.

Mr Smith	*Risk Score*
Male	1
Systolic pressure 210	4
Diastolic pressure 115	2
Smokes 30 cigarettes a day	5
3 relatives with heart disease	6
Blood cholesterol 7.3 mmol/l	6
Quetelet Index 3.237	2
Total	26

26 points = high risk

Advice: Mr Smith should read the following chapters and act on the advice given in them. He should then re-assess his risk index in three months time.

Worked example 2

Miss Jones, blood pressure 110/73, smokes 5 cigarettes a day. She has
no relatives with angina or who had a heart attack under the age of
55. Her blood cholesterol level is 7.1 mmol/l, her height is 5′2″ and
her weight is 8st 3lb.

$$\text{Calculation of Quetelet Index} = \frac{\text{Wt (kg) x 1,000}}{[\text{Ht (cm)}]^2}$$

$$\text{Weight 8st 3lb} = 52.2 \text{ kg}$$

$$\text{Height } 5'2'' = 156 \text{ cm}$$

$$\text{Quetelet Index} = \frac{52.2 \text{ x } 1,000}{(156)^2}$$

$$= \frac{52,200}{24,336}$$

$$= 2.145$$

Thus Miss Jones's Quetelet Index is less than 2.75.

Miss Jones	*Risk Score*
Female	0
Systolic pressure 110	0
Diastolic pressure 73	0
Smokes 5 cigarettes a day	1
Blood cholesterol 7.1 mmol/l	6
Quetelet Index 2.145	0
Total	7

7 points = moderate risk

Advice: Miss Jones should read the following chapters. She should pay
special attention to stopping smoking and reducing her blood cholesterol
level. She should re-assess her index in three months time.

SUMMARY

- You may calculate your own risk of suffering a heart attack using the cardiovascular risk score table on p.30.

- If your risk score is moderate, elevated or high, read the following chapters and act on the advice contained in them.

- Repeat your risk score in three and six months' time to make sure that it has gone down. All factors, except being male and your family history, may be lowered by following the instructions.

- Repeat your risk score every year and ensure that it does not creep up with time.

4
How to Reduce Your Own Risk of a Heart Attack

THE STORY SO FAR . . .

Chapters 1-3 have introduced you to the massive problem of heart disease, outlined the known risk factors, and allowed you, with the help of your GP, to make an assessment of your present risk of a heart attack. You should also have identified which particular risk factors may be high in your case and require special attention.

The next six chapters are devoted to strategies to lower each risk factor. Chapter 11 is written for the heart attack patient, and tells you how you can adjust after a heart attack and prevent a recurrence. Chapter 12 gives a description of general practice screening for heart disease, and Chapter 13 tells you how to resuscitate someone after a heart attack.

No doubt readers will wish to pay particular attention to the chapters dealing with the risk factors to which they are particularly susceptible and may even consider missing out 'non-relevant' chapters; for example, non-smokers may think that there is no interest for them in Chapter 5 on how to stop smoking. However, even this chapter has a section on passive smoking which is of importance to all non-smokers sitting next to a smoker and inhaling his or her fumes.

The rest of this chapter is devoted to some important basic principles concerning heart disease.

WHY PEOPLE GET HEART ATTACKS

The reason people get heart attacks (especially at a young age) is because there is a fundamental mistake in the way they live their lives. They probably have one or more of the risk factors: smoking, high blood pressure, raised blood fats, obesity, diabetes, lack of exercise, family tendency to heart attacks, excess stress, personality type, high alcohol intake and gout. People who have few or none of these risk factors would be most unlucky to get a heart attack.

A heart attack, however, should not be seen as a completely negative event, but rather as the body's way of compensating for some unsatisfactory factor in the lifestyle. The body may react to this factor by giving the patient a severe chest pain, forcing him or her to go to bed and withdraw from work and society (ie to stop smoking, reduce excess stress and drinking, and stop overeating). If nature's lesson is not learnt at this stage, and if there is no modification in lifestyle to cut out the problem factor(s), then it is likely the same disease will recur (ie there will be a further heart attack).

Thus is is not a satisfactory response to race back to work immediately after a heart attack, and continue to live in the same fashion as before. The heart attack has shown that this lifestyle is flawed.

VAGUE ILLNESSES AND HEART ATTACKS

A large proportion of patients attending their general practitioners are unable to define their problem precisely. They complain of vague symptoms with descriptions of 'feeling off', 'under the weather', 'tired and no energy'.

To understand the reason for this, it is helpful to look at the several stages that any disease goes through, as shown in the scale of health below:

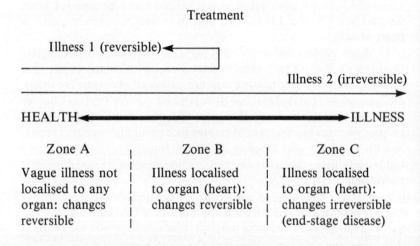

The figure above gives the range of health/illness, from complete health, at the left-hand side of the diagram, to complete illness, at the right-hand side of the diagram. In the first stage of disease (Zone A), the illness is vague and cannot be localised to any one organ. At this stage it is reversible. The disease may then get worse and move into

Zone B. It may then be localised to a particular organ, in this case to the heart giving pains (often mistaken for indigestion), shortness of breath and sweating; at this stage the disease is still reversible. If no further steps are taken to modify and improve the lifestyle then the illness becomes irreversible, remaining localised to the heart and causing angina and/or a heart attack.

The ideal time to act is when the disease is in Zone A or Zone B when it is still reversible and a full recovery is possible (as in Illness 1 above). In comparison, treatment of irreversible disease in Zone C (end-stage disease) is difficult and perfect results cannot normally be obtained (as in Illness 2 above).

THREE-POINT PLAN TO AVOID A HEART ATTACK
(or recover after a heart attack)

You will need to tailor your personal health programme to your own personality, lifestyle and situation. You must treat the 'whole person' (both *mind* and body) rather than just treating one organ or symptom: the affected organ is merely the 'weak link' in your body and is the first to protest on behalf of the whole body at some unsatisfactory feature(s) of your lifestyle. If you continue to live the same way, the symptoms (angina) from that organ (the heart) will get worse (become a heart attack), or else move to another organ (eg the brain to produce a stroke).

The three-point plan is:

1. Reduce your TOTAL LOAD of risk factors.
2. Particularly reduce the risk factors to which you are especially susceptible.
3. Plan a recovery programme of diet, rest and relaxation, exercise and sleep, with vitamin supplements.

Reducing your total load
If you have five risk factors, and each can be reduced by 10%, then that will give a large overall reduction in risk and this may be enough to allow the body to recover. It is the TOTAL LOAD of risk factors that is so important and at the onset of illness, a small rise in just one of the risk factors is the straw that breaks the camel's back.

The effect of the total load is, to an extent, subjective and depends on your standpoint. The patient may imagine his load to be greater than it actually is, whereas an outsider may perceive the patient's load as less than it is, thus causing further stress to the patient.

Reducing risk factors to which you are especially susceptible
This is another feature of tailoring your personal health programme
to your own situation. There is enormous variation in the initial state
of health from person to person, and in their ability to recover from
a disease-inducing risk factor(s), such as cigarette smoking, diet, stress
or alcohol. For example, in one individual stress may cause high blood
pressure, whereas in another individual with a similar lifestyle the blood
pressure is unaffected.

Your recovery programme
A proper diet, rest and relaxation, regular physical exercise, adequate
sleep (eight hours a night) with vitamin supplements where necessary
(vitamin B compound, vitamin C and vitamin E) are invaluable in returning to health.

SUMMARY

● Work out a personal health plan.

● Tailor your personal health plan to your own personality, lifestyle
  and situation and treat the 'whole person' (mind and body).

● Reduce your TOTAL LOAD of risk factors.

● Particularly reduce the risk factors to which you are especially
  susceptible.

● Plan a recovery programme of proper diet, rest and recovery,
  exercise and sleep, with vitamin supplements.

5
How to Stop Smoking

There is now increasing evidence for the view that the single most important risk factor for heart disease is smoking. This fact is of special importance since smoking is a risk factor that can be completely eliminated.

In other words, if you were thinking of smoking — DON'T!

Smoking not only causes heart attacks but many other diseases including strokes, cancer of the lung, throat and bladder, chronic bronchitis and emphysema, duodenal ulcers, blood clots in the legs and lungs, and a vast range of less serious but troublesome diseases and conditions. The medical profession have no doubt of the dangers of smoking and the Royal College of Physicians of England and the Surgeon General of the USA have both pronounced smoking as the major cause of illness and premature death in modern western society.

SMOKING AND HEART ATTACKS — THE FACTS

The British Heart Foundation has stated that if the entire population of the UK gave up smoking there would be 10,000 less men and women of working age dying of heart attacks each year.

Previously, a large proportion of doctors used to smoke but when the dangers of cigarettes became obvious, the vast majority gave up. Studies showed that smoking doctors, aged 35 to 44, had five times the risk of a heart attack compared to non-smoking doctors, and smoking doctors aged 45 to 54 had four times the risk of heart attacks compared to non-smoking doctors.

Smoking reduces your life expectancy, as shown by the following statistical details:

● Men aged 25 who have never smoked will have a life expectancy of six and a half years more than smokers.
● Men who smoke and inhale 20 cigarettes per day from age 20 will reduce their life expectancy by 20% to 25%.
● Men who smoke 40 or more cigarettes a day can expect to reduce their life expectancy by 14 to 15 years.
● Women who smoke 40 or more cigarettes a day can expect to reduce their life expectancy by 19 to 20 years.

WHY DO PEOPLE SMOKE?

Smoking is a learned behaviour. No one in Britain smoked before 1586 when Sir Walter Raleigh (inadvisably) brought tobacco back from America — there is no historical evidence to suggest that the population of England suffered from not smoking prior to this date.

Smoking is promoted, or at least not actively discouraged, in society, perhaps because of the staggering finances involved.

It is estimated that in 1986 the British Treasury received £5,737 million from tobacco duty and VAT on cigarettes. However, the Consumer Consultative Council have in the past estimated that, although the tax revenue from tobacco is enormous, it repays only approximately one-third of the cost to the country of smoking comprising: NHS treatment for smoking related illnesses (£500 m); 50 million working days lost through smoking; sickness and invalidity benefit; widows pensions, and the cost of fires and accidents.

Although there has been pressure on successive governments from interested bodies to ban smoking, or at least make it prohibitively expensive (eg £5 for a packet of 20 cigarettes, with the extra duty received by the Treasury spent on the NHS), so far these moves have been unsuccessful.

Amazingly, approximately 70% of adult smokers would like to give up smoking but only approximately 30% are able to do so. To understand why this peculiar situation occurs it is instructive to see why people start, and then continue to smoke.

WHY DO PEOPLE START SMOKING?

Smoking behaviour is often learned at a surprisingly young age, and studies have shown that children of 10 to 13 years have already begun to think about smoking, even if they have not actually started. Children are greatly influenced by the media, and although smoking adverts on television are now banned and smoking has been discouraged in TV films and plays, tobacco sponsorship of televised sports events is allowed and adverts in magazines and on public hoardings are all permitted. These all give the strong message that a smoker will in some way (usually undefined) be more attractive, mature, adult, sophisticated and successful.

The propaganda has been successful, especially on young women, who now have the highest rate of starting to smoke. This is particularly alarming, since these young women are more susceptible to the dangers of tobacco smoke than other groups, and also since smoking causes many problems with conception, pregnancy, breast feeding and the oral contraceptive.

The children who are most likely to start smoking are those who are more precocious and physically mature for their age, and especially those who are resentful of authority figures, eg teachers and parents. They see smoking as a way of confirming their own maturity and independence and striking back against such authority figures.

WHY DO PEOPLE CONTINUE SMOKING?

Once someone has started smoking, they are then likely to continue, despite the feeling that they would like to give up. This is because they are physically and mentally addicted, and they feel smoking gives them some social acceptance and companionship. Many smokers see their activity as a solution to their problems of anxiety, lack of confidence, boredom and inability to concentrate, and feel that it helps them solve their problems or calm them after a bad experience.

A large proportion of smokers do try to give up smoking at some stage, and there is an initial success rate of some 70% to 80%, but the long-term success rate is only 20%. There is a strong case for society to make far more resources available to help people give up smoking and stay off cigarettes. Suggestions for this would include:

- better patient education of the dangers of smoking
- stop-smoking clubs (Smokers Anonymous)
- making nicotine chewing gum available on the NHS
- banning all cigarette advertising and tobacco sponsorship of sporting events.

No single method of stopping smoking is outstandingly successful, and the reason for this low long-term success rate is probably because the smokers are tackling the wrong problem. The real problem is *not*:

'How do I give up smoking?
but
'What factors and problems cause me to smoke, and how can I alter these and then give up smoking?'

In other words, trying to give up smoking, without altering the situation and problems that cause the smoking behaviour, is unlikely to be successful.

The way to decide why you smoke is to analyse your smoking behaviour by using a 'smoking diary' (as on the next page). This will identify the places, activities and reasons for smoking and help you to build up a realistic plan to stop.

ANALYSIS OF REASONS FOR SMOKING

There is a vast range of possible reasons why a person smokes, but it is helpful to classify these under some broad headings which then will help greatly in selecting the most suitable method of giving up. It is the *reason* for smoking that primarily needs to be examined, and when this is found and tackled then the desire to smoke will probably become much less and easier to cope with.

Craving or addictive smoking

This type of smoking does not occur until a person has been taking cigarettes for some time, and it is a true addiction, possibly as strong as an addiction to heroin. The smoker will have an exceptionally powerful desire to smoke, and believe that he or she cannot go on another moment without a cigarette when the craving starts.

Characteristic of this type of smoking behaviour is the enormous lengths to which a deprived smoker will go to get a cigarette after shops have closed. Once such a smoker has experienced the situation where

Smoking Diary	Day:				Date:	
Time	No. of cigarettes	Place	Activity	Reasons why you smoked (a-e)	Importance of cigarette (1-4)	Comments
0-7 am 7 am 8 am 9 am 10 am 11 am 12 noon 1 pm 2 pm 3 pm 4 pm 5 pm 6 pm 7 pm 8 pm 9 pm 10 pm 11 pm 12 pm						
	Total cigarettes					

Instructions:

- Mark each cigarette smoked as x.
- Note down place and activity whilst cigarette smoked (also preceding problem if relevant).
- Note reason why you smoked cigarette and its importance to you from the alternatives below.

Reason for smoking (arousal level):

(a) craving for cigarette
(b) felt tense or anxious
(c) needed stimulation or lift to get going or concentrate
(d) habit — automatic smoking — 'I was unaware I was doing it'
(e) to relax or enjoy whilst relaxing

High arousal

Low arousal

Importance of cigarette (desire to smoke):

(1) Slight desire: 'I was unaware I was smoking it'.
(2) Moderate desire: 'I could have done without it'.
(3) Great desire: 'I needed that cigarette'.
(4) Very great desire: 'My life depended on having that cigarette'.

Make any other relevant comment that may help you analyse your behaviour, eg 'I always have to smoke when I drink coffee, see the boss, am worried'.

they have run out and have no cigarettes, they will take many precautions always to keep a supply of cigarettes in reserve or, alternatively, coins for a cigarette machine in order to avoid the severe physical and mental withdrawal symptoms.

Addictive smokers have two problems:

1. the initial difficulty that led them to continue smoking, and
2. the withdrawal symptoms caused by stopping smoking.

The first problem must be sorted out, and then, in order to stop addictive smoking, suitable substitutes need to be found. Friends and relatives should be enlisted for mental and emotional support together with the removal of as many as possible of the trigger factors and trigger behaviours. The smoker should also find suitable rewards for non-smoking behaviour. One of the best times to stop addictive smoking is when you are ill, and have a greatly reduced desire to smoke.

Tension, anxiety or stress smoking

This is one of the commonest reasons for people to smoke. The smoker finds that he or she is made anxious by some person or factor, and they initially smoke as a way (they think) of tranquillising themselves, although the smoking actually has the opposite effect of making them more tense and raising their pulse and blood pressure. Often an anxious person will want to start fiddling with something, and the smoking gives them a ritual of opening the packet, taking out the cigarette, putting it in the mouth, lighting a match and inhaling a deep breath

of smoke. This activity may also give the smoker an extra ten seconds to think when confronted by an anxiety-provoking situation.

The way to deal with this type of smoking is to deal with the anxiety-producing factor in some other way. Learn a relaxation technique such as deep breathing, exercise, or have a substitute ready, such as a piece of fruit or a mint to eat, or something else to fiddle with such as keys, pencils, string, worry beads or a toothpick. When the anxiety is successfully dealt with, the desire to smoke will be enormously reduced.

For other ways of coping with stress see Chapter 9.

Stimulation smoking

This is the smoking behaviour associated with boredom. These smokers feel they need a 'lift' to get them through the day or help them concentrate on the activity in hand. They smoke when they are feeling low or depressed as a way to pick themselves up.

The cigarettes keep the smoker 'hyped' up, but the answer is to use some more natural stimulant such as physical exercise, deep breathing, talking to friends, changing activity, or listening to the radio or music. If you feel swamped with work, then plan to take a few hours break and return refreshed without the need for cigarettes.

Habit smoking

This is almost an automatic process. The smoker is often not even aware of the fact that they are smoking. They light one cigarette after another, without being conscious of how many cigarettes they are getting through.

A 'smoking diary' is especially useful to reveal this sort of pattern. Alternatively, keeping the cigarettes in an unusual place or not bringing any matches will also reveal habit smoking. Very commonly, smokers light up automatically after certain trigger factors and trigger behaviour, such as after a meal, with tea, coffee or alcohol, on the telephone, or whilst occupied watching TV or reading a book.

Relaxation smoking

Many smokers use smoking as an aid to relaxation, or smoke when they are feeling relaxed. Once they have completed some task, or are having a drink of tea, coffee or alcohol at a break, they reach for their cigarettes since they consider that they will be much calmer with a cigarette.

To stop relaxation smoking, you should find some other pleasurable way of relaxing that does not include smoking. If you do want to smoke then make sure you don't relax and enjoy it — try standing outside in the cold, or sitting on a hard chair in an unpleasant environment.

THE BENEFITS OF GIVING UP SMOKING

As any good salesman knows, in order to sell any item or plan you must first be able to promise some benefits. This is particularly the case when you ask yourself to give up smoking as you may also encounter physical and mental problems caused mainly by the withdrawal of nicotine. These symptoms include:

- initial nervousness and goose-pimples ('cold turkey')
- lethargy

- headaches
- sore throats and breathlessness
- weight gain.

However, the good news is that these withdrawal symptoms are usually only temporary and will normally disappear within two weeks of stopping smoking.

You will need to see both the short-term and long-term benefits of giving up smoking to encourage you to overcome the initial problems and continue to abstain.

Short-term benefits

- You will rapidly be able to breathe more easily and be able to exercise far longer and harder. If you already suffer from angina, then this condition will probably be improved and may even disappear completely.
- You will regain your sense of smell and taste.
- Your breath, clothes and hair will no longer smell like an ashtray.
- Your teeth and gums will become much healthier.
- Your skin will improve especially on the face. It is usually possible to recognise a smoker by looking at the skin over the angle of the cheek: in a non-smoker, the uppermost layer of skin is, as a rule, fine and translucent whereas in a smoker it is more coarse and opaque.
- You will have more disposable income. (For a person smoking 20 cigarettes a day, this would be around £12 a week, £600 a year, or £24,000 in a smoking lifetime.)

Long-term benefits

- There will be a dramatic improvement in your chances of reaching and enjoying retirement. The risk of a heart attack disappears rapidly soon after stopping smoking, and after avoiding cigarettes for one year the risk of having a heart attack drops by 50%. After five to ten years the heart attack risk of an ex-smoker is about the same as that of a non-smoker.
- If you smoke five or more cigarettes a day, and suffer a heart attack, then stopping smoking at this point will reduce your risk of a further heart attack sevenfold.

STOP SMOKING PLAN

This consists of three parts:

1. Having read the first part of this chapter and analysed what sort of smoking behaviour you have and what your underlying problems are, you should now work out how to sort out those underlying problems, and also which strategies from the following pages you would like to use.
2. Choose a day two to three weeks ahead, make a note yourself, and tell other people that you are going to give up smoking on that day.
3. Enlist the support of others, and avoid trigger factors and trigger behaviour.

Look at the following lists of alternatives to select strategies and activities that will assist you, underlining those you intend to use.

These stratagems are for people who want to give up completely:

● **Identify the problems which cause you to continue smoking.**

● **Remove the trigger factors and trigger behaviour.** Change your routine and avoid or reduce all factors and behaviour that trigger smoking such as stress, anger, coffee or alcohol (try tonic water instead), and social situations and parties with other smokers (don't accept cigarettes!). Avoid personal crises, stressful holidays and contact with other smokers in the early stages.

● **Find substitutes for smoking.** These may be either activities or objects. Exercise, especially breathing exercises, and social contact will divert your attention away from smoking and there are many activities that can keep the hands or the mouth busy such as toothpicks, mouthwashes and chewing mints or gum. Go for a walk after a meal. Take a shower before breakfast and a warm bath at night.

● **Gain mental and emotional support from yourself and others.** Mentally prepare yourself to give up smoking by setting some date in advance, then tell others. Overcome your fears and objections to stopping smoking. See yourself as a non-smoker. Don't apologise for not smoking. Ask friends and relatives to help you through the withdrawal symptoms.

● **Reward yourself for non-smoking behaviour.** For example, put aside the money saved from smoking for some other non-smoking (preferably non-fattening) treat.

For those smokers who wish to give up gradually (and usually unsuccessfully) these extra stratagems may be added.

● **Make it more difficult to smoke.** Make your cigarettes and/or lighter less accessible by hiding them, putting them in a drawer, pocket or another room. Some smokers try the nuisance approach of changing brands with every new pack, and putting out a cigarette after each puff, or else leaving it in the ashtray. Others do not let themselves smoke whilst doing another activity, for example, watching television, eating, reading or drinking, and if they wish to smoke they must stop the other activity. Other smokers make certain rooms or times non-smoking and deliberately go to places where smoking is not allowed, eg sitting in the non-smoking part of a bus, train or restaurant.

● **Employ delaying tactics.** Increase the time between cigarettes: one hour in the first week, two hours in the second week, and so on. Cut out the 'easy' cigarettes first by not smoking before breakfast or one hour before bedtime, and gradually increase the non-smoking period.

● **Reduce the dose of nicotine.** Smoke only half a cigarette and do not inhale. Ration yourself to a certain number of cigarettes a day, or try a pipe or cigar but don't inhale. Change to a lower nicotine content cigarette, and allow only one cigarette after a meal or one cigarette per hour. Drink lots of water to flush out the nicotine.

When you have read the rest of this chapter come back to this Stop Smoking Plan and re-read it. GOOD LUCK!

OTHER TECHNIQUES

There are other techniques to help you stop smoking. Some of them help the underlying problems of tension or anxiety but all these techniques still require a high motivation to persevere with not smoking.

Aversion therapy
The basis of this technique is to associate smoking with some nasty experience, for example, to make yourself physically sick through oversmoking (eg smoking three cigarettes as fast as possible), or to associate smoking with some unpleasant situation. There is also a preparation available which makes a cigarette taste horrible.

Hypnosis
Although it is suggested that giving up smoking can be assisted by self-hypnosis, to have a good chance of success it is very important to go to a skilled therapist who will be able to suggest to you whilst you are in a hypnotic trance that you don't wish to smoke any more. However, for this method to work you must truly want to give up smoking.

Deep breathing

This can often be coupled with a form of self-hypnosis and can lead to a state of deep relaxation, after which the desire to smoke is much less. This technique is far more successful when taught by an experienced practitioner.

Acupuncture

This is often helpful for the heavy smoker on more than 20 cigarettes a day. A needle or stud is placed in the earlobe on the acupuncture point corresponding to the lung. The needle or stud is then twirled and this in some way appears to reduce the desire to smoke. The stud is left in the earlobe for up to two weeks and twirled by the wearer whenever the (hopefully) ex-smoker has the desire to restart.

Nicotine chewing gum (Nicorette)

This is a substitute for smoking. A smoker using this method should stop all cigarette smoking completely and solely use the chewing gum. It has the advantage of occupying the mouth, and as the gum is chewed nicotine is absorbed directly from the mouth, thus mimicking the effect of smoking.

Each piece of gum lasts for up to 30 minutes; when the chewing stops the nicotine is no longer released. The gum is deliberately designed not to taste too pleasant so that you will not become addicted to the chewing gum instead.

After a short period of stabilisation, the number of pieces of gum chewed per day is slowly reduced until it is completely stopped.

The gum should not be used during pregnancy, and those with dentures may find it difficult to chew. Regrettably, this gum is not available on the NHS.

PASSIVE SMOKING

It has only recently been realised that non-smokers may be harmed by the cigarettes smoked by people around them. This passive smoking especially occurs in small rooms and confined spaces which have poor ventilation. The smoker pollutes the air with a high concentration of carbon monoxide and carcinogens, especially benzopyrene, which the unwitting non-smoker takes in to his or her lungs. It has been shown that such passive smokers have a high incidence of smoking-induced diseases.

To reduce health risks to non-smokers, smoking ideally should be banned from public places, buildings, restaurants and transport, as has already happened in many places in the USA. In addition, employees working particularly in open plan offices should be given the chance to vote on whether they wish to allow smoking at work. If the majority do not wish to allow it, the employer should implement a 'no smoking' policy and set aside one or two rooms (not the eating areas) where smoking is permitted.

WHAT ABOUT CIGAR AND PIPE SMOKING?

Cigar and pipe smoking is slightly less harmful than cigarette smoking for at least three reasons:

- The smoke path in the cigar and pipe is longer than that in a cigarette, and filters out more of the dangerous substances.
- Cigar and pipe smokers tend to inhale less and to keep the cigar or pipe in the hand and not in the mouth.
- Cigars and pipes go out when not actively smoked, since the tobacco is made without the sodium nitrate which is put into cigarettes to make them burn continuously.

However, most of the comments in this chapter apply also to cigar and pipe smoking and the advice is the same — **don't do it!**

SUMMARY

Key points for the individual about smoking:

- The single most important risk factor for heart attacks is smoking. Stopping smoking reduces dramatically the incidence of heart attacks and increases life expectancy.
- Smoking is a mental and physical addiction, and can be beaten only after a very positive and committed decision to give up.

- Smoking is usually a sign that the smoker has some other problem, eg anxiety, boredom, inability to relax, which must be solved in a way other than smoking.

- The main factor dictating the success of a 'stop smoking' plan is whether or not the individual is highly motivated to persevere with the plan.

- The target of any no-smoking plan is to stay off cigarettes for the rest of your life. Face the fact that this means you must never take another cigarette. The first six to twelve months are the most critical.

- Be realistic and choose a method that suits you.

Key points for society about smoking:

- The price of cigarettes could be raised substantially, and the extra duty received by the Treasury spent on the NHS (a 'smoking tax').

- Tobacco advertising and sponsorship of events could be phased out within the next five years.

- Smokers who wish to give up could be given more assistance.

- Greater steps could be taken to avoid passive smoking in public places and at work.

6
How to Reduce Raised Blood Pressure

After stopping smoking, one of the best ways to guarantee a long and healthy life is to ensure that you do not suffer from raised blood pressure. High blood pressure damages the blood vessels, and in England and Wales arterial disease (heart attacks and strokes) is responsible for about 40% of deaths in both men and women. It is often said that high blood pressure (together with haemorrhoids, varicose veins and income tax) is the price we pay for the western way of living: the disease is almost unknown in primitive rural civilisations.

BLOOD PRESSURE CRITERIA

The heart is an intermittent pump, ie it pumps one beat and pauses while the chambers refill. There is, therefore, a variation in blood pressure, the maximum pressure being called the **systolic** and the minimum pressure being called the **diastolic.** This pressure is usually measured in millimetres (mm) of mercury (Hg).

The World Health Organisation's criteria for blood pressure are:

'Normal' blood pressure = 100-140 mm Hg systolic
                          60- 90 mm Hg diastolic

'Borderline Raised' blood pressure = 140-159 mm Hg systolic
                                     90- 94 mm Hg diastolic

'Raised' blood pressure = greater than 160 mm Hg systolic
                                       95 mm Hg diastolic

It used to be thought that the diastolic (minimum) blood pressure (which reflects the resting pressure in the heart muscle wall in between beats) was the more important, and raised blood pressure is therefore usually assessed in terms of the level of this figure. More recently, however, it has been appreciated that the systolic (maximum) blood pressure is also an important indicator of likely damage caused by raised blood pressure.

The criteria usually used for assessing raised blood pressure are:

	Diastolic	
95-105 mm Hg	=	mild raised blood pressure
105-120 mm Hg	=	moderate raised blood pressure
Greater than 120 mm Hg	=	severe raised blood pressure

BLOOD PRESSURE AND HEART ATTACKS

There is no 'safe' blood pressure below which it is impossible to sustain a heart attack. However, as blood pressure rises so does the risk of a heart attack. For example, someone with raised blood pressure of 160/95, aged between 30 and 59 years, will probably have about three times the risk of a heart attack compared with a person with normal blood pressure (together with seven times the risk of a stroke and four times the risk of heart failure).

Raised blood pressure encourages heart attacks by accelerating the rate at which deposits of fat (atherosclerosis) form in the heart arteries; it causes strokes by causing small blow outs (aneurysms) in the arteries of the brain. Not surprisingly, high blood pressure in a younger person is more worrying as it has a longer timespan in which to damage the arteries.

MEASUREMENT OF BLOOD PRESSURE

Most adults have had their blood pressure measured at some time in their life. It is an easy and painless procedure, and can easily be learnt by almost anyone. If you buy your own blood pressure machine and stethoscope you can carry it out yourself at home (make sure the cuff on the machine is the right size for your arm). The procedure is as follows:

1. The patient is made comfortable, and a cuff wrapped around the upper arm keeping the forearm level with the heart.

2. The mercury column is put up to the vertical (not necessary with aneroid or electronic blood pressure machines but these are less accurate).

3. The cuff is inflated until the radial pulse disappears (see p.128).

4. The cuff is deflated at a rate of 2 mm of mercury drop per second, whilst a stethoscope is used to listen over the area of the brachial artery. When a sound first appears that is the systolic blood pressure.

5. The cuff is allowed to continue to deflate, and when the sound becomes muffled, that is called the '4th' point. When the sound disappears completely that is the '5th' point. In Britain the diastolic is measured as the '5th' point (in USA the diastolic is the '4th' point).

Blood pressure may be measured while sitting, standing, lying or after exercise, but the most common is in the first position. The blood pressure will probably rise after stress, anxiety or tension (including attending the doctor), after a large meal, coffee, exercise or smoking. There is also a variation at different times of the day, blood pressure being highest at 9.00 am and lowest at 4 am (the greatest number of heart attack deaths occurring in the middle of the night). The blood pressure goes up slowly with age in western civilisation, although this rise does not occur in China, India and parts of Africa.

CAUSES OF RAISED BLOOD PRESSURE

Somewhat surprisingly, no known cause can be found for high blood pressure in 90% of cases. Blood pressure may often be reduced by attention to lifestyle (eg obesity control, care with diet and salt, coffee and alcohol intake, cigarette smoking, exercise and stress management).

It is likely that raised blood pressure can be inherited, but families with high blood pressure tend to share not only the same genes but also the same diet, environment and habits, so it is not easy to separate nature from nurture.

However, there is now little doubt that raised blood pressure is encouraged by the lifestyle of the average city dweller: many studies, especially those carried out in the Third World, have shown a dramatic rise in blood pressure when country dwellers move to the city.

The remaining 10% of raised blood pressure is due to a wide variety of causes including pregnancy (the raised blood pressure of pregnancy is often called pre-eclamptic toxaemia), kidney disease, rare tumours which secrete substances that raise blood pressure, certain congenital malformations such as narrowing of the main vessel of the body (co-arctation of the aorta), and the side effects of drugs, eg steroids, the oral contraceptive pill, alcohol and certain antidepressants.

INVESTIGATION OF RAISED BLOOD PRESSURE

Raised blood pressure is usually SILENT, although in a small proportion of cases when the blood pressure is very high there may be symptoms such as headaches, dizziness, breathlessness, palpitations, ankle swelling, nose bleeds, noises in the ears, unusual memory loss and fatigue. Raised blood pressure is often first found at a routine medical examination, eg for insurance purposes, but increasingly it is being detected by cardiovascular screening carried out at a GP's surgery (see Chapter 12).

Before raised blood pressure is treated, it is first necessary to confirm that it is truly present by taking several readings. Initially, blood pressure is checked 5 minutes after the first estimation and if it is still raised the patient is asked to return on another occasion for rechecking. If the blood pressure persists at the raised level it is usual to carry out some baseline investigations to try and establish its cause.

The threshold after which raised blood pressure should be investigated is:

> Aged 20-65 years   90-100 mm Hg diastolic
> Aged 65 + years   100-110 mm Hg diastolic

The baseline investigations are in three parts:

- **The history:** The doctor asks the patient many questions to try and establish the likely cause of the raised blood pressure, and to see if there may already be silent complications. Special attention is paid to factors mentioned above, with questions about the health of close family members.
- **Examination:** The doctor examines the patient's body to look for signs of high blood pressure and its complications. Special attention is paid to the heart, brain and kidney.
- **Special investigations:** The urine is tested for the presence of sugar (for diabetes) and protein (for kidney disease). Urine is also sent

to the local laboratory to see if any germs can be grown from it, and to see if there are any unusual cells to be found under the microscope. Blood tests are taken to look for anaemia and any problems with the kidney or salt concentration. The chest is X-rayed to show possible heart enlargement. An ECG is taken to show if there is any heart strain, or if the patient has suffered any previous undetected heart attacks. The kidneys are X-rayed (called an intravenous pyelogram — IVP or IVU) to show possible kidney abnormalities. A sample of all urine passed in a 24-hour period is collected to look for raised levels of substances associated with tumours that raise blood pressure.

CRITERIA FOR TREATMENT

Once raised blood pressure has been identified, a careful decision must be taken whether or not to treat it and what the most satisfactory method might be. For the 10% of cases where there is a traceable cause it may be possible to treat this problem, for example, pregnancy is self limiting, kidney disease or infection may be treated, rare tumours may be surgically removed, congenital malformations of arteries may be corrected, and drugs producing side effects can be stopped.

The object of any treatment should be to reduce blood pressure to less than 105 mm Hg diastolic, and treatment is particularly required if:

- the diastolic is greater than 120 mm Hg;
- the raised blood pressure starts when the patient is aged less than 40 years;
- there are already complications such as angina, heart disease or strokes, kidney disease and brain tumours; and
- there is a family history of any of the above or sudden death.

Raised blood pressure is more common in women than in men, but is more serious in men than women.

BLOOD PRESSURE TREATMENT IN BRITAIN

The treatment of blood pressure is not one of medicine's success stories, as reflected in the 'Rule of Halves'. Approximately 20% of the British population suffer from hypertension, of which only half (c. 10%) are detected. Of the detected half, only one half of these (c. 5%) are treated, and of the treated half, only half (c. 2½%) are treated adequately. In other words, one eighth of the total number of raised blood pressure cases are properly treated.

There is a large regional variation in the level of high blood pressure in Britain, with generally lower levels found in the more affluent areas and in the South East, and higher levels in the less affluent areas and in the North and West.

The regional variation in deaths from heart attack is very similar to the distribution of raised blood pressure with the greatest number of deaths centred around Belfast and Glasgow.

REGULATION OF BLOOD PRESSURE

The level of blood pressure is regulated by two factors:

1. the amount of blood pumped out by the heart (**cardiac output**), and
2. the resistance to blood flowing around the body (**peripheral resistance**) which occurs at the level of the small arteries.

The blood pressure can be expressed by the formula:

Blood pressure = Cardiac output x Peripheral resistance

The cardiac output is dependent on the pulse rate (**heart rate**), and the volume of blood expelled with each heart beat (**stroke volume**) or:

Cardiac output = Heart rate x Stroke volume

Normal blood pressure is regulated by these three variables (heart rate, stroke volume and peripheral resistance), and these factors are controlled in a complex way by nerves, hormones and other chemical substances circulating in the blood.

Usually the first change to occur in raised blood pressure is a rise in cardiac output, and then after some time there is a secondary rise in peripheral resistance, and the cardiac output drops back to normal.

TREATMENT

The non-drug and drug treatments for high blood pressure work by acting on one or more of these three factors (heart rate, stroke volume, peripheral resistance), thus reducing blood pressure to lower and safer levels.

Non-drug treatment

This is most certainly the preferred way since it will probably involve reversing the factors that may have caused the raised blood pressure in the first place (ie raised blood pressure due to increased cardiac output and increased peripheral resistance). Non-drug treatments include stress management (see Chapters 9 and 10), reducing weight and alcohol intake (see Chapter 8), stopping smoking (see Chapter 5), reducing dietary salt (sodium chloride), increasing exercise (see Chapter 10), and possibly avoiding soft drinking water (see Chapter 8). The simple stratagems, where appropriate, of reducing salt intake or losing five kg (11 lb) in weight can bring about a blood pressure reduction of about 10 mm of mercury diastolic with a consequent major improvement in life expectancy.

Drug treatment
Despite the increased risk of a heart attack and strokes from raised blood pressure, drug treatment is not to be entered into lightly because:

● High blood pressure is usually silent and without symptoms, but many of the treatments cause side effects which can severely and adversely affect the quality of life. Powerful drugs can cause powerful side effects, and although more modern drugs have fewer side effects than their predecessors, there is no point taking a drug if its side effects are worse than the disease it is attempting to treat.

● Blood pressure medication once started (apart from for pre-eclampsia of pregnancy) will need to be continued for life. It is very important to take the blood pressure medication as directed, since suddenly stopping the medication may cause problems.

Once a patient with raised blood pressure has had baseline investigations, the doctor or hospital consultant will decide on a suitable treatment. Non-drug methods should be started, supplemented with suitable tablets if necessary. The medication prescribed will depend on how high the blood pressure is raised, and if there is insufficient improvement the medication will be increased in dose or changed for stronger medication.

Drugs used in the treatment of raised blood pressure
All drugs in Britain are given three names: a chemical name, an approved name and a brand name. The chemical name is rarely used except by organic chemists, the approved name or generic name is the name used in the section below, and the brand names are the ones the manufacturer has selected for his product, and are usually the easiest of the three to remember. If you are taking medication for blood pressure you will be able to find the approved name on the bottle, usually in smaller letters below the brand name, and by reading the following sections you will be able to see how it reduces your blood pressure.

Drug treatment is usually commenced if there is a blood pressure of 105-115 mm mercury diastolic, especially if the patient is less than 65 years and has any other complications of hypertension or family history of problems with high blood pressure, heart attacks or strokes. If the blood pressure is greater than 115 mm mercury diastolic, then urgent treatment is particularly important.

Diuretics

Amiloride	Frusemide
Bendrofluazide	Hydrochlorothiazide
Bumetanide	Indapamide
Chlorothiazide	Methylchlorothiazide
Chlorthalidone	Polythiazide
Cyclopenthiazide	Spironolactone
Ethacrynic acid	Triamterene

Diuretics work on the arterial walls and on the kidneys, reducing circulating blood volume: thus both the peripheral resistance and cardiac output are reduced. They are effective for mild raised blood pressure, especially in old people, but initially cause a high urine output, which may be inconvenient. They also encourage the likelihood of diabetes, gout and may reduce blood potassium level. Male impotence is a concerning side effect.

Beta-blockers

Acebutolol	Oxprenolol
Atenolol	Pindolol
Betaxolol	Propanolol
Lebetalol	Sotalol
Metoprolol	Timolol
Nadolol	

These work on the heart, small artery walls and kidneys, reducing both cardiac output and peripheral resistance by changing the body's response to circulating adrenalin. They are particularly useful in patients under 40 years, where they bring about a 10-15% reduction in blood pressure in 75% of cases. They work far less well in old people (60 years or over).

The well recognised side effects of beta-blockers are getting tired quickly after exercise, cold hands and feet, and setting off heart failure and asthma attacks in patients with known weaknesses in these areas. They tend to slow the heart (to about 60 beats a minute) and may mask the symptoms of a low blood sugar (hypoglycaemic) attack in a diabetic.

Beta-blockers do seem to reduce the level of fatal heart attacks in non-smoking men with high blood pressure.

There are slight variations in how the different beta-blockers affect the heart, lungs and brain, and how many times a day they have to be taken, but your doctor will pick the most suitable one for your case. Beta-blockers alone are used for mild to moderate raised blood pressure.

Beta-blocker and diuretic combinations

Acebutolol and hydrochlorothiazide
Atenolol and chlorthalidone
Timolol and hydrochlorothiazide amiloride
Metoprolol and chlorthalidone
Metoprolol and hydrochlorothiazide
Nadolol and bendrofluazide
Oxprenolol and cyclopenthiazide
Pindolol and clopamide
Propranolol and bendrofluazide
Sotalol and hydrochlorothiazide
Timolol and bendrofluazide

These work on cardiac output and peripheral resistance. The two drugs may be successful if combined when individually they have been unsuccessful. Combination therapy is used for moderate to severe raised blood pressure.

Vasodilators

Hydralazine   Prazosin   Minoxidil

These act by reducing peripheral resistance, and sometimes cause a reflex increase in the heart rate. Consequently, they often need to be used with a beta-blocker which stops this reflex increase. They may have potent side effects, but they are of value because in cases of very high blood pressure they may be life saving.

Calcium antagonists

Diltiazem   Nifedipine   Nicardipine
Lidoflazine   Verapamil

These drugs affect the way that the muscle cells use calcium, and reduce both cardiac output and peripheral resistance. They are used especially if angina is also present. The side effects of headaches, flushing, peripheral oedema and constipation may occur. It is important not to take a beta-blocker with verapamil or diltiazem without close medical supervision.

ACE inhibitors (angiotensin enzyme converting inhibitors)
Captopril   Enalapril   Lisinopril

These reduce peripheral resistance by stopping the process that makes angiotensin (which causes high blood pressure). They can be life saving, but must be used with care in patients with kidney disease: often a test dose is given first. ACE inhibitors are particularly effective when used with a diuretic.

Centrally acting hypertensive drugs
Alpha methyldopa   Clonidine

These operate in different ways, and even after many years of use are still not fully understood. They are not much used now, apart from methyldopa, which despite a large number of potential side effects seems safe when treating asthma, heart failure and pre-eclamptic toxaemia of pregnancy.

Other drugs
Bethanidine   Guarethidine   Reserpine
Debrisoquine

These drugs have many, often severe, side effects and consequently are rarely used in modern blood pressure therapy.

Taking your medication
Important rules for patients on tablets to reduce raised blood pressure are:

- Use non-drug methods to reduce blood pressure wherever possible.
- Take your tablets as prescribed.
- Do not run out of tablets or stop them without instructions.
- Attend your doctor for regular checks as requested.
- Report side effects.
- Don't take any other non-prescribed drugs (even over-the-counter drugs like aspirin) since they may cause interaction with your medication.
- Always remind your doctor that you have raised blood pressure before starting any new tablets, having an operation or general anaesthetic, or visiting the dentist, since your raised blood pressure may alter the treatment given.

SUMMARY

- Raised blood pressure usually gives no symptoms, but is a major risk factor for heart attacks and strokes.

- There is no safe blood pressure level below which there is no risk of a heart attack, but the World Health Organisation has defined raised blood pressure as:

  greater than $\dfrac{160 \text{ mm mercury (systolic)}}{95 \text{ mm mercury (diastolic)}}$

- The causes for raised blood pressure cannot be found in 90% of cases, but could well be due to the pressures of city life.

- The object of blood pressure treatment is to reduce the diastolic to below 105 mm mercury. However, only one eighth of the total number who suffer from high blood pressure in Britain are adequately controlled.

- The initial treatment for raised blood pressure is without drugs, but if this fails then drugs should be taken for life as directed by the doctor.

7

How to Reduce Your Blood Fat Levels

A raised level of blood fat is one of the three major risk factors for heart attacks. There are two sorts of fat in the blood, **cholesterol** and **triglyceride.** These fats will not dissolve in water and so they need to be bound in special carrier substances, called **lipoproteins,** in order to be transported by the blood.

There are four types of lipoprotein (fat carriers) as shown in Fig. 6:

- **HDL (high density lipoprotein)** — usually carries approximately a quarter of the circulating cholesterol
- **LDL (low density lipoprotein)** — usually carries approximately three-quarters of the circulating cholesterol
- **VLDL (very low density lipoprotein)** — carries triglycerides at all times
- **Chylomicron** — carries triglycerides immediately after meals; absent from blood between meals.

Fig. 6

CHOLESTEROL

Cholesterol is needed by the body to make cell walls, bile and hormones. The liver produces approximately 1 g (1/27th of an ounce) of cholesterol per day; however, all the cells of the body are able to make it. A small amount of cholesterol (0.3 g per day) is absorbed from the gut irrespective of the amount eaten, but a high fat diet causes the body to make more cholesterol and the blood level goes up.

The HDL (high density lipoprotein) and LDL (low density lipoprotein) have opposite functions: the HDL removes cholesterol present in the blood and vessel walls (where it may encourage heart attacks) and returns it to the liver where it can be broken down and excreted. The LDL (low density lipoprotein) does the opposite, and transports cholesterol from the liver around the body, encouraging the deposition of cholesterol into the blood vessel wall, with consequent narrowing of the artery as shown in Fig. 7.

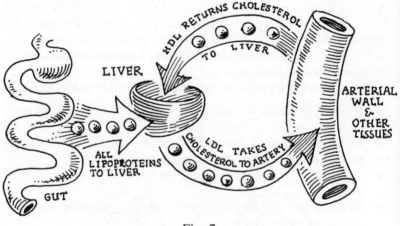

Fig. 7

Foods which raise blood cholesterol include meat, especially offal, dairy products, eggs and shellfish. The blood cholesterol level does not vary much during the day and it is not necessary to fast to get an accurate level of cholesterol.

TRIGLYCERIDES

The main source of blood triglycerides is dietary fat. The western intake is usually much greater than the body's requirements, for example, in the USA the daily fat intake is 60-150 g (2½-6 oz), whereas in the Third World it is 30-40 g (1-1½ oz) a day — and heart attacks are much less common amongst the latter population.

Triglycerides are stored in fat cells, and released when necessary as an important source of energy. The level of triglycerides is related to eating and varies enormously before and after meals; in order to find an accurate blood triglyceride level it is necessary to fast for 12-14 hours before having blood taken.

RAISED BLOOD FATS AND HEART ATTACKS

Heart attacks are caused by two related processes:

● The first is a long-term one in which a fatty substance called **atheroma** is deposited in the lining of the heart arteries causing a narrowing of the vessel. This process frequently starts in childhood, and is related to the level of blood fats, especially the LDL cholesterol fraction. In general terms, the higher the level of blood fats the more rapidly the atheroma is deposited into the wall of the vessel. This process is symptomless, and may have reached quite an advanced stage with over half the cross sectional area of the artery blocked before the patient is aware of any problem.

● The second process causing a heart attack is a sudden one in which a **thrombus** (or clot) is deposited onto the already damaged wall of the artery of the heart, causing a complete blockage, and thus not allowing blood to flow through. If the heart muscle is starved of blood for more than about half an hour it dies, and this causes a heart attack (see Fig. 8).

ATHEROMA

ATHEROMA + CLOT

Fig. 8

The rate of formation of atheroma is related to smoking, raised blood pressure and also to the circulating level of cholesterol (especially LDL cholesterol), and probably to a lesser extent to the triglyceride level. The rate of thrombus formation is related to a raised triglyceride level and an increased tendency of the blood to clot.

The Framingham Study carried out in Massachusetts, USA found a strong relation between raised levels of cholesterol and increased risk of heart attack, as set out in the following table:

Blood cholesterol level	*Likelihood of heart attack*
Less than 5.01 mmol/l	1
5.01-5.63 mmol/l	1.5
5.63-6.4 mmol/l	2
More than 6.4 mmol/l	2.5

This is confirmed by British figures, which suggest that men whose blood cholesterol level is greater than 7.2 mmol/l have three times the risk of a heart attack compared with men with a cholesterol level of less than 5.5 mmol/l. Also the typical British male (with a median cholesterol level of 6.2 mmol/l) has twice the risk of a heart attack compared with someone with a lower cholesterol level of around 5.5 mmol/l. In other words, 60% of middle-aged British men are at risk of a heart attack due to raised cholesterol, and only 15% of adult men in Britain have cholesterol of less than 5.0 mmol/l which could be considered a safe level.

Factors known to raise blood cholesterol levels are:

- Diet, especially foods high in cholesterol and saturated fats (see Chapter 8)
- Smoking
- Stress
- Inactivity
- Family history of high cholesterol (hypercholesterolaemia — see below)
- Being male
- Diabetes
- Sugar
- Coffee (more than 8 cups a day)
- Thyroid hormone deficiency (myxoedema)
- Obstruction of the bile duct (joining the liver to the gall bladder)
- Kidney disease
- Normal pregnancy.

The HDL (high density lipoprotein) cholesterol level is particularly important, since it appears to be 'cardio-protective'. It reduces the number of heart attacks by returning cholesterol from the heart artery walls to the liver for excretion. Consequently, heart attacks are more than twice as common in people with an HDL cholesterol level of less than 0.93 mmol/l compared to people with HDL cholesterol levels of 1.06 mmol/l or greater.

Taking regular aerobic exercise causes an increase in HDL cholesterol, and lowers the incidence of heart attacks.

Encouraging news
It has been demonstrated that if the blood level of cholesterol is reduced the incidence of heart attacks goes down. In one study a 1%
drop in cholesterol level was associated with a 2% drop in heart attacks. In an American study carried out between 1961 and 1973, the
number of men with a serum cholesterol level of greater than 6.7 mmol/l
dropped by 13% and the number of women by 23%. During this time
there was an astounding drop in heart attacks of 30%: strong encouragement to the whole population to take steps to reduce their cholesterol
level and thus the overall rate of heart attacks.

Hereditary raised blood cholesterol (familial hypercholesterolaemia)
This occurs in the population in one in every 500 (about 100,000 people
in Britain) and is the commonest single gene-inherited abnormality (ie
a failure of one gene to work correctly). It is associated with a high
circulating LDL cholesterol level, and this causes a very high rate of
heart attacks.

If both parents suffer from this disease, some of their offspring will
suffer from a double dose of the fat metabolism defect (called
homozygous familial hypercholesterolaemia). It is usually fatal before
the age of 15.

However, the far more common, single-dose fat metabolism defect
(called heterozygous familial hypercholesterolaemia) usually causes
heart attacks from the age of 20 onwards. Without adequate treatment
half the males suffering from heterozygous familial hypercholesterolaemia will die before the age of 60.

The way to diagnose this condition is to look for lumps in the ten-
dons (tendon xanthoma), especially in the Achilles tendon and fatty
lumps (ganglia) on the back of the hands. The condition also causes
accumulations of fat in and around the eye.

This condition should be suspected in any family where members have
died from heart attacks before the age of 55 years. If you are worried
that you may have this condition, you should consult your GP who
can arrange for you to have your blood fats measured without charge
at an NHS hospital. There is also a patient help group called The Family
Heart Association (see p.148), which publishes leaflets and advises about
inherited tendencies to develop high blood fats.

TRIGLYCERIDES AND HEART ATTACKS

It is likely that raised triglyceride levels may also cause heart attacks.
A clue to the importance of triglycerides has come from the observa-
tion that Eskimos have a very low incidence of heart attacks, and also

very low triglyceride levels. A typical Eskimo triglyceride level is 0.64 mmol/l compared to the United Kingdom range of 1-1.5 mmol/l.

Raised triglycerides probably encourage heart attacks by speeding the formation of atheroma, and making the blood more likely to clot.

Raised triglyceride levels may be due to rare inherited disorders of metabolism (see the Frederickson Classification table on p.73) in which blood triglycerides are too high (greater than 4 mmol/l). However, far more commonly, a raised triglyceride level is a secondary symptom of some other factor or disease, including:

- Diet ⎫ These are by far the commonest causes of raised
- Obesity ⎭ triglyceride levels. See Chapter 8 for details of how to treat obesity.
- Diabetes mellitus
- Alcohol intake
- Gout
- Thiazide diuretics ⎫ Drugs used to reduce
- Beta-blockers ⎭ raised blood pressure.
- Oral contraceptives
- Thyroid hormone deficiency (myxoedema)
- Kidney disease
- Liver disease
- Metabolic and endocrine disorders
- Acute stress eg burns.

To achieve an accurate triglyceride level, it is important to take a blood sample after twelve to fourteen hours of fasting.

FINDING YOUR CHOLESTEROL AND TRIGLYCERIDE LEVELS

Go to your GP and ask for this test. It is available without charge on the NHS, and there is now a strong case for every adult to have their blood fats measured at least once in their lifetime.

Your GP may take the blood himself, or arrange for you to go to your local hospital. You will have to fast for fourteen hours before the blood is taken in order to get an accurate result of your triglyceride level.

Many fat disorders do not show themselves until early middle age, although serious problems can be detected from 1 year of age.

You should have this screening test particularly if you have or are:

- A family history of raised blood fats
- A history of heart attacks or strokes in close family before the age of 55 years
- A smoker
- High blood pressure
- Overweight and have a sedentary job
- Diabetes mellitus
- Gout.

ADVISABLE LEVELS OF BLOOD FATS

Unfortunately, there is no totally safe level of cholesterol below which heart attacks will never occur. However, to all intents and purposes, anyone with a cholesterol level of less than 5.2 mmol/l, who does not have a raised blood pressure and who is not a smoker would be most unlikely to have a heart attack before retirement age.

The European Atherosclerosis Society have suggested guidelines for blood fat levels:

Target blood fat levels: Cholesterol: less than 5.2 mmol/l
Triglyceride: less than 2.3 mmol/l

However, if your cholesterol and triglyceride levels are above these, or if your cholesterol level alone is greater than 6.5 mmol/l irrespective of the triglyceride level, then it is important to improve your level of blood fats by a change of lifestyle (diet, losing weight and exercise). If your cholesterol level is greater than 7.8 mmol/l, you may have to use a lipid lowering drug.

HOW TO REDUCE BLOOD FATS LEVELS

This is a process that should start in childhood, because atheroma starts as soon as your blood fats are too high. The three main principles are:

1. Control of obesity — see Chapter 8 (see calorie guides on pp.83-85
    — select as much as possible of your diet from Table A);
2. Adequate vigorous aerobic exercise — see Chapter 10;
3. Reduction of fat intake by attention to diet.

Here are some guidelines:

*   Reduce your fat intake by a quarter (so that only 30% of your dai-
    ly calories are obtained from fat).
*   Take more polyunsaturated fats (from vegetable sources: liquid at
    room temperature). Reduce saturated fats (from animals: solid at
    room temperature). You should aim for a ratio of polyunsaturated
    fats to saturated fats of 0.45 (in other words, try to make sure that
    approximately half of all your fat intake is from vegetable sources
    and liquid at room temperature).
*   Reduce intake of meat, dairy products, eggs, shellfish, sugar and
    salt.
*   Increase intake of fibre, especially wholemeal bread and oats, raw
    fruit and vegetables, fish and chicken. It has been found that high
    levels of dietary fibre are able to reduce cholesterol levels.
*   Substitute skimmed milk for full cream milk and cottage cheese
    for hard cheese. Allow yourself only 2 eggs per week.
*   Change your cooking habits: have your food grilled, poached or
    boiled rather than fried. Cut all the visible fat off meat before
    cooking.

With these measures you can hope to reduce your cholesterol level by
about 15%.

Role of the food industry

The food industry has a vital part to play in the prevention of heart
disease by reducing the fat, sugar and salt content of food. Lower fat
meats and low-salt bread are already available in other countries and
similar foods could be promoted and made widely available in Britain.
All packaged foods could be labelled with an analysis of protein, carbohydrate, fat, salt and calorie content.

   If these measures were combined with a programme of nutritional
education, the British public would be better informed to find an alternative to the present diet of 'chips with everything'.

DRUGS USED TO TREAT FAT ABNORMALITIES

Before considering drug treatment (and having eliminated other reasons
for raised blood fats, such as diabetes and thyroid disease), your doc-

**Hereditary Blood Fat Abnormalities (after Frederickson),
with their dietary and drug treatments**

Type	Fat abnormality	Comment	Dietary treatment (after attaining ideal weight)	Drug treatment
I	Triglyceride raised	Rare inherited disease. No increased risk of heart attack	Low fat diet	None available
IIa	Cholesterol raised	Heart attack risk greatly increased	Low saturated fat diet	Ion exchange resins, fibrates, nicotinic acid, probucol
IIb	Cholesterol and triglyceride raised	Heart attack risk increased	Low saturated fat diet	Nicotinic acid and ion exchange resins, fibrates
III	Cholesterol and Triglyceride	Heart attack risk greatly increased	Low saturated fat diet	Fibrates, nicotinic acid
IV	Triglyceride raised	Heart attack risk increased	Carbohydrate restriction	Fibrates, nicotinic acid
V	Triglyceride raised	Heart attack risk usually increased slightly	Low fat diet with carbohydrate restriction	Fibrates, nicotonic acid, fish oil

tor will try to get your blood fat levels down by the use of diet, exercise and obesity control. He will be aiming for target levels of cholesterol less than 6.5 mmol/l and triglyceride less than 2.3 mmol/l with the above dietary measures.

However, it is estimated that 5-10% of the British population might need treatment with fat lowering drugs. The table on p.73 uses the Frederickson Classification to describe hereditary fat abnormalities and gives an assessment of the likely risk of a heart attack for each abnormality. Approximately 90% of inherited blood fat abnormalities are of types IIa, IIb or IV. Types I, III and V are rare.

Drugs which lower the cholesterol level only

Ion exchange resins (cholestyramine and colestepol)
These work by reducing the amount of LDL cholesterol by 25-35%, which is achieved by disrupting normal bile metabolism.

Usually the liver uses cholesterol to make bile salts, which are needed for the absorption of cholesterol from the gut. The bile salts are secreted into the gut to aid digestion and then re-absorbed. Ion exchange resins bind the bile acids within the gut and they are not then re-absorbed. The liver is forced to use its own cholesterol to make more bile acids, with a consequent reduction in the level of LDL cholesterol in the blood.

However, although this is a useful drug, sometimes side effects such as bloating, flatulence and constipation can prevent its continued use. There can also be drug interaction and reduced vitamin and folic acid absorption.

Probucol
The action of this drug is unknown, and it works solely on cholesterol. However, it may reduce HDL cholesterol as well as LDL cholesterol.

Drugs which lower both cholesterol and triglyceride levels

Fibrates
These are bezafibrate, gemfibrozil and clofibrate. Fibrates can all lower cholesterol (by up to 20%), and triglycerides (by 30-50% or more). LDL cholesterol tends to fall and HDL cholesterol tends to rise. It is not known how these drugs work, and, although they are well tolerated with few side effects, the long term safety of their use is unknown.

Nicotinic acid

The action of this drug is unknown. However, it does reduce LDL cholesterol and triglyceride. It has the side effect of flushing and gastrointestinal symptoms, although the former can be blocked by aspirin. It also causes problems in patients suffering from diabetes, gout and liver disease.

Drugs which lower triglyceride levels

Fish oil extract (eicosapentaenoic acid)

This is highly effective in reducing grossly raised triglyceride levels and also the likelihood of the blood to form clots. It seems to be very safe apart from an interaction with tablets that thin the blood (oral anticoagulants).

Other drugs

Statins (HMG-CoA reductase inhibitors)

This is a new class of drugs, already enthusiastically used in America although at present unavailable in the UK. They are very effective in reducing LDL cholesterol from the circulation by increasing the number of 'LDL receptors'. The statins work even better when used in conjunction with an ion exchange resin and together they can cause a reduction in LDL cholesterol of up to 70%.

Other drugs that may affect blood fat levels

Some drugs used to treat raised blood pressure, angina, diabetes, and for contraception may adversely affect the circulating level of blood fats. For example, betablockers decrease the level of the cardioprotective HDL cholesterol, and thiazide diuretics increase the level of the dangerous LDL cholesterol.

SUMMARY

● Raised blood fats are a major risk factor for heart attacks. The higher your cholesterol level the greater your risk.

● All adults should have their blood fat level measured. The target levels are:

> Cholesterol: less than 5.2 mmol/l
> Triglyceride: less than 2.3 mmol/l

- Blood fats may be reduced by correct diet, control of obesity and vigorous aerobic exercise.

- The food industry has a valuable part to play in reducing fat, sugar and salt consumption, and should consider labelling all packaged foods with a full analysis of content.

8
How to Control Your Weight and Diet

THIS CHAPTER WILL HELP YOU TO LOSE WEIGHT WITHOUT TEARS!

Being overweight (obese) is very common and in the UK approximately:

1 man in 5
}
1 woman in 3
is overweight

THE HEALTH PROBLEMS OF BEING OVERWEIGHT

People who are heavier than their ideal weight are more likely to suffer from high blood pressure, raised blood fats, diabetes and gout, all of which increase the risk of a heart attack. This is reflected in life expectancy statistics:

- If you are over 25% overweight your life expectancy is likely to be shortened by 3.6 years.
- If you are 35% overweight your life expectancy is likely to be shortened by 4.3 years.
- If you are 45% overweight your life expectancy is likely to be shortened by 6.6 years.
- If you are 55% overweight your life expectancy is likely to be shortened by 11.4 years.

HOW OBESITY STARTS

Childhood

Obesity often begins in childhood. Overweight parents tend to have overweight children, and these children tend to grow up to become overweight adults themselves, thus completing the cycle. In contrast, normal weight parents tend to have normal weight children.

- Families with normal weight parents: approximately 10% of children are overweight.
- Families with one parent overweight: approximately 40% of children are overweight.
- Families with two parents overweight: approximately 80% of children are overweight.
- 80% of overweight children become overweight adults.
- 50% of extremely overweight adults were overweight children.

Although being overweight may be a problem inherited from parents, it is much more likely that the children merely learn their parents' conspicuously bad eating habits (ie they eat the wrong foods and consume too many calories).

Adolescence
During this stage in life, most youngsters seem to be able to eat large quantities of high calorie foods, crisps, chips, ice cream and chocolate, without putting on weight. This is due first to the fact that they are usually very physically active and at school take part in organised games, and secondly their bodies have a greater ability to reset their rate of metabolism to burn up excess calories rather than convert them into fat. This latter facility is reduced later in life, and so weight gain starts in the majority of adults at around age 25.

On the other hand *obese* adolescents cannot eat in the same way as their contemporaries without putting on weight, and on average are less physically active.

Adulthood
Once you have become an overweight adult, it can be very difficult to lose those excess pounds. An overweight person may eat no more than a normal weight person, and still not lose weight (is there no justice?). Also, there is a great deal of misinformation and misdirection relating to diets, and after failing to lose weight, many dieters, not surprisingly, lose heart. Weight loss by crash diets is usually unsuccessful, because they tend to do just that . . . CRASH!!

Crash diets
Many crash diets ignore the way the body works. When you severely limit your calorie intake (less than 1,000 calories per day) there is a 'fasting effect' and the body automatically resets the rate of metabolism at a very low level so that your calorie requirements are small. As a result, while fasting, you will often feel lethargic, depressed and have no energy. (This ability of the body to lower the rate of metabolism

enables the body to survive when food is scarce.) When you stop the diet, whether after a day's fasting or two weeks of not eating, the rate of metabolism is still set at a low level. So, it is likely that even a normal meal will have more calories than you require, causing a rapid and demoralising weight gain.

Approximate calorie requirements by age

	Male	Female
Adolescent	3,000	2,200
Young adult	3,000	2,100
Middle aged adult	2,500	2,000
Old aged adult	2,300	1,800

These figures are approximations, and a person weighing more than average will require slightly more calories and vice versa.

Excess food calories are converted into body fat (1 lb of body fat = 3,500 calories). The problem with weight gain is that the effect is cumulative, and a small daily excess, say of 100 calories (equivalent to ½ ounce of butter or 1 can of cola), will cause a weight gain of approximately 1 lb per month, 12 lb a year, or over 4 stones in 5 years.

YOUR IDEAL WEIGHT

The way to tell if you are overweight is to look at the tables on page 80 and compare your weight for your height with the ideal ones.

HOW TO LOSE WEIGHT WITHOUT TEARS

● Analyse your eating habits using the 'diet diary' (see p.82). This will help you to identify the situations and factors that encourage eating.
● Modify your existing eating habits *for the rest of your life*. By following some relatively simple basic principles you will know what to eat and how much to eat while still enjoying your food, and thus lose weight without suffering. However, weight loss is a long-term strategy and you must plan ahead. By using the method described, you can expect to lose 1-2 lb a week until you reach your target weight. There is no one diet that will work for everyone, nor only one personality type that can be successful in losing weight. The secret is, as in any medical treatment, to tailor the cure to the patient, or the new eating habits to the individual.
● Decide on a daily calorie allowance, and divide it into meal allowances (eg 1,000 calories a day — breakfast 300 calories, lunch 350 calories, evening meal 250 calories, drinks and other meals 100

HEIGHT AND WEIGHT TABLES
MALE

Maximum desirable weight for men aged 25 plus
Instructions: Weigh yourself in indoor clothing wearing shoes.
Subtract 8 pounds (3.6 kg) if naked

Height without shoes		Body frame						
		Small			Medium		Large	
ft in	m	st lb	kg	st lb	kg	st lb	kg
5 3	1.60	8 9	55	9 7	60	10 4	65
5 4	1.63	9 0	57	9 10	62	10 8	67
5 5	1.65	9 3	59	9 13	63	10 12	69
5 6	1.68	9 7	60	10 3	65	11 2	71
5 7	1.70	9 11	62	10 7	67	11 7	73
5 8	1.73	10 1	64	10 12	69	11 12	75
5 9	1.75	10 5	66	11 2	71	12 1	77
5 10	1.78	10 10	68	11 6	73	12 6	79
5 11	1.80	11 0	70	11 11	75	12 11	81
6 0	1.83	11 4	72	12 2	77	13 2	84
6 1	1.85	11 8	74	12 7	80	13 7	86
6 2	1.88	11 13	76	12 12	82	13 12	88

FEMALE

Maximum desirable weight for women aged 25 plus
Instructions: Weigh yourself in indoor clothing wearing shoes.
Subtract 5 pounds (2.25 kg) if naked

Height without shoes		Body frame						
		Small			Medium		Large	
ft in	m	st lb	kg	st 'lb	kg	st lb	kg
4 11	1.50	7 3	46	7 12	50	8 10	55
5 0	1.52	7 6	47	8 1	51	8 13	57
5 1	1.55	7 9	49	8 4	53	9 2	58
5 2	1.57	7 12	50	8 7	54	9 5	60
5 3	1.60	8 1	51	8 10	55	9 8	61
5 4	1.63	8 4	53	9 0	57	9 12	63
5 5	1.65	8 7	54	9 4	59	10 2	65
5 6	1.68	8 11	56	9 9	61	10 6	66
5 7	1.70	9 0	58	9 13	63	10 10	68
5 8	1.73	9 5	60	10 3	65	11 0	70
5 9	1.75	9 9	61	10 7	67	11 4	72
5 10	1.78	10 0	64	10 11	69	11 9	74

calories). If you wish to lose weight, your daily intake *must be less* than your daily energy expenditure.
● Increase your energy expenditure by exercise.

HOW TO ANALYSE YOUR EATING HABITS

To do this, you will need to keep a diet diary (see p.82). When you fill this in, you will be amazed at how much you eat and drink (especially when you count calories).

For each food fill in the number of calories which you will find in the table. In the comment column you can note where you ate and what made you hungry, eg smell or sight of food, it was lunchtime, hunger pains, headaches, dizziness, comfort-eating due to anxiety, loss of control when seeing food, feeling stressed or emotional which encouraged eating, etc.

Use the diary to see what situations and factors make you eat, and when and where you were eating. Then you can find stratagems and substitutes to avoid the situations and factors which make you want to eat. In many cases the *real* reason for overeating (like smoking) is some other problem which needs to be sorted out first, after which weight loss becomes relatively easy.

CALORIE GUIDE

Tables A-C on pages 83-85 give the calorie content of some common foods. All values are given for 1 ounce of food, except where mentioned (1 oz = 27 g). Try to select as much as possible of your diet from Table A (Low Calorie Foods). You will find these more filling, but less fattening. Weigh foods on kitchen scales until you get used to judging portions. The calorie guides have been prepared on the basis not only of the number of calories but also the nutritional value of each food item (cholesterol, salt, sugar, fibre and protein content).

MODIFYING YOUR EATING HABITS

Once you have identified when, where and what you eat, you will be in a much better position to change your eating habits. Count calories to ensure you don't have more than you need. Concentrate on *quality* of food rather than *quantity*.

Your diet should consist of as many of the low calorie foods in Table A as possible, with Table B foods taken in moderation.

Diet Diary	Day	Food	Date	Drink	Weight	Calories	Comment
Time							
7.00 am							
8.00 am							
9.00 am							
10.00 am							
11.00 am							
12 noon							
1.00 pm							
2.00 pm							
3.00 pm							
4.00 pm							
5.00 pm							
6.00 pm							
7.00 pm							
8.00 pm							
9.00 pm							
10.00 pm							
11.00 pm							
12 m'night							

Table A (Low Calorie Foods: mostly fruit and vegetables)
(Calories per oz)

Food	Cal	Food	Cal	Food	Cal	Food	Cal
Apple	10	Cress	2	Mixed vegetables (frozen)	18	Raspberries (fresh)	8
Apricots (fresh)	8	Cucumber	3	Mushrooms (raw)	3	Rhubarb (raw)	3
Asparagus	5	Damsons (raw)	8	Mustard and Cress	2	Satsuma	8
Banana	13	Fish (steamed)	30	Onion (raw)	10	Soup (clear)	1
Beans (runner)	3	Fruit juice (no sugar)	12	Orange	8	Soya sauce	5
Beetroot	8	Grapefruit	3	Orange juice (no sugar)	11	Spinach	8
Blackberries (fresh)	8	Grapes	15	Parsnips (boiled)	15	Sprouts (boiled)	5
Broccoli	4	Horseradish sauce	1	Peaches (fresh)	9	Strawberry (fresh)	8
Bran	17	Leeks	8	Pear (fresh)	9	Swedes (boiled)	5
Cabbage	3	Lemon	3	Pepper (green)	6	Tangerines	8
Carrots (boiled)	5	Lettuce	3	Pickled onions	5	Tea (lemon, 1 cup)	1
Cauliflower	3	Loganberry (fresh)	5	Pineapple (fresh)	2	Tea (milk, 1 cup)	20
Celery	3	Mackerel (boiled)	35	Porridge	4	Tomatoes (fresh)	4
Cheese (cottage)	24	Marmite	2	Potatoes (boiled)	23	Tomato juice	6
Cherries (fresh)	11	Melon	4	Radishes	5	Turnips	3
Cod (steamed)	22	Milk (skimmed)	10			Watercress	4
Coffee (black, 1 cup)	15					Yoghurt (low fat)	12
Coffee (milk, 1 cup)	24						

Table B (Moderate Calorie Foods: mostly lean meats and carbohydrates)
(calories per oz)

All Bran	88	Cream crackers	40	Kippers	58	Prawns	30
Apple chutney	60	Curried beef	32	Lobster	34	Prunes (dried)	38
Apricots (dried)	50	Curried chicken	32	Macaroni (boiled)	33	Rice (boiled)	35
Avocado pear	25	Custard	33	Marmalade	70	Rice pudding	43
Beans (baked)	25	Egg (boiled)	45	Meusli	105	Shepherds pie	33
Beef (minced)	50	Egg (scrambled)	79	Milk (whole)	19	Shrimps	33
Beef steak (grilled)	86	Figs (dried)	60	Mousse	55	Soup (thick)	25
Blancmange	35	Fish cake	63	Omelette (plain)	58	Spaghetti (boiled)	27
Bread (brown)	70	Fish (fried)	60	Peas	18	Sweetcorn	26
Chicken (boiled)	55	Fish (fingers, 1)	55	Pickles	40	Tomato sauce	20
Chicken (roast)	55	Fruit cordial	30	Potato (jacket)	30	Tuna	50
Coleslaw	43	Gravy (thin)	35	Potatoes (instant		Turkey	55
Corn (cob)	28	Herring (fried)	65	mashed)	35	Veal	66
Cottage pie	32	Jam	70	Potato salad	23	Yoghurt (fruit)	20
Crab	37	Jelly	37				

NB: Always try to eat unrefined (brown) rather than white carbohydrate, eg brown bread, brown rice, wholemeal macaroni and spaghetti.

Table C (High Calorie Foods: mostly fats)
(Calories per oz)

Food	Cal	Food	Cal	Food	Cal	Food	Cal
Apple fritter	50	Chocolate (plain)	155	Liver (fried)	78	Raisins (dried)	70
Bacon	175	Cocoa	120	Margarine	220	Rice (fried)	45
Beefburger	101	Coffee (milk, sugar, 1 cup)	75	Mayonnaise	90	Salad cream	111
Beef (roast, fat)	109	Cornflakes	104	Milk (condensed)	100	Sausage	85
Beer (pint)	160	Cornflour	100	Mince pie	110	Scampi	50
Biscuits (digestive, 1)	60	Cream (double)	130	Oatmeal	115	Scones	105
Biscuits (shortcake, 1)	50	Cream (single)	60	Olive oil	260	Scotch egg	75
Brazil nuts	185	Custard tart	82	Pancakes	85	Soft drinks (1 can)	100
Butter	220	Dates	70	Pastry	162	Spirits	70
Bun (cream)	97	Doughnut	100	Pasty	66	Sugar	110
Bun (currant)	87	Fat (cooking)	260	Pâté	205	Sweets	95
Cake (cream)	100	Flour	100	Peanuts	170	Tea (milk, sugar, 1 cup)	75
Cake (fruit)	107	Gravy (thick)	50	Peanut butter	180	Treacle tart	107
Cereals (breakfast)	100	Ham (fat)	123	Pizza	52	Trifle	42
Cheese (cheddar)	120	Honey	80	Pork	129	Wine	80
Cheese (cream)	230	Jam tart	110	Pork pie	110	Xmas pudding	100
Cheese (slices)	98	Lamb chop	143	Potatoes (chips)	68	Yorkshire pudding	63
Cheese (spread)	80	Lemon curd tarts	125	Potatoes (crisps)	165		
Chocolate (milk)	165			Potatoes (roasted)	35		

NB: Current research suggests that oatmeal may have a beneficial effect on blood cholesterol levels.

Generally you should avoid high calorie foods in Table C. However, if you particularly like one high calorie food *plan* to allow yourself a small amount of that food, which you can then enjoy far more. Avoid other high calorie foods that you are not particularly keen on.

Be prepared for temptation, and particularly avoid situations that make you overeat. For example:

● At social events and parties, especially where there is alcohol, develop strategies that allow you to take control of your eating. Drink mineral water, not alcohol, and at a buffet, first view all the food available, then take a small plate and serve yourself on the basis of your preferred list of low calorie foods. If you especially want it, treat yourself to a *small* amount of an item from Table C high calorie foods.

● Being anxious, overtired or overstressed is a common reason for overeating. Appreciate that you are comfort eating, and try to find a suitable substitute or a stress reducing stratagem (see chapters 9 and 10).

● If you're the sort of person who likes to nibble while watching television, make a point of turning the set off whenever you want to eat.

● To lose weight, take three small meals a day, and do not miss breakfast. Each meal encourages the 'thermogenic effect' (the opposite of the 'fasting effect'), and after eating the metabolism is set at a higher than normal rate. This encourages the burning up of calories, and also explains the 'lift' you feel after a small to medium size meal. People who stop smoking tend to gain weight, because smoking previously stimulated the thermogenic effect.

● Weigh yourself naked at the same time each day, and keep a record of weight loss (there is a weight loss chart for you to use at the back of the book). Look at *overall* trends, and do not worry too much about day-to-day variation. You can vary several pounds from day to day solely due to water retention.

- Keep a picture of yourself at a better weight, and look at it when you feel hungry. Also try imagining yourself the size of your refrigerator and instead of eating take a drink of water.

- Don't eat if you are just slightly hungry, but rather learn to enjoy your hungry feeling since it means you are losing weight. However, don't allow yourself to get ravenously hungry or fast for too long, since the thermogenic effect is then lost. Eat more slowly, chewing your food, and always take time to eat your meal properly or else postpone it until later. Eat more fresh fruit, vegetables or wholemeal bread and fish (increasing your intake of dietary fibre) and reduce the level of fats, salt and sugar. Keep a banana or apple by you as a low calorie snack instead of eating a chocolate bar.

- Eat your food restaurant style, serving yourself but leaving the bowls in the kitchen not on the table which encourages you to eat more. Prepare less food and eat less at each meal. Eat a banana 20 minutes before your meal to reduce your appetite. Reward yourself for weight loss with something that you particularly want, such as some new clothes.

EXERCISE

Exercise is dealt with in greater detail in Chapter 10, but here are some general rules in relation to weight loss.

- Exercise is almost always helpful in a weight loss plan.
- Exercise promotes loss of fat and conserves lean tissue, ie important body proteins, like muscles.
- In the average person, physical activity can burn up approximately one-third of the daily calorie intake. Increasing physical activity consequently increases the number of calories burned up with subsequent fat loss.
- The most successful form of exercise to help you lose weight is **aerobic exercise:** this is activity vigorous enough to make you sweat and breathe more quickly, raising your pulse rate. It should be carried out for at least 20 minutes, two to three times a week.
- Exercise elevates mood and often reduces hunger.

OTHER METHODS OF WEIGHT REDUCTION

Appetite suppressants

These work by suppressing the desire to eat, and in the short term can produce moderate weight loss. This is usually short lived, and when the tablets are stopped weight is frequently regained very rapidly because eating habits have not been altered. Many of these tablets are related to amphetamines, and most are controlled drugs. They cause sleep disturbances and their long-term safety is unclear.

Surgery

There are basically three sorts of technique for the treatment of obesity:

1. *Wiring the jaw shut.* This forces the patient to take only liquids through a straw, which is far more difficult than eating in the normal way. For example, 2,000 calories is equivalent to five and half pints of milk. Consequently this method usually causes a large short-term weight loss . . . until the jaw is unwired when the weight is frequently regained very rapidly since eating habits have not been re-educated.

2. *Stomach volume reduction.* The capacity of the stomach is reduced, by filling it with a balloon, or else gathering the stomach wall into a pleat with staples. This operation is reversed after the desired level of weight loss is achieved, by which time the patient has probably become used to eating less at each meal.

3. *Bypass operations.* There are many different techniques, but the underlying principle is that the digestive tract is short-circuited.

Thus, instead of food passing through 20 feet of small intestine and 5 feet of large intestine (a process taking 24 to 48 hours during which all but 5% of the nutrients are absorbed), the food is given a much shorter course (in both length and time) and many of the calories and nutrients are not absorbed. Weight loss is rapid and permanent until the surgery is reversed.

However, there is a high price to pay for this benefit including persistent diarrhoea, possibly severe deficiency disease (due to the body's inability to absorb sufficient vitamins and minerals from the shortened bowel), and sometimes even death.

OTHER DIETARY FACTORS

Diabetes and diet

There are about half a million cases of diagnosed diabetes in Britain, and probably a similar number of undiagnosed patients. Diabetes is due to a partial or complete lack of the hormone **insulin,** and is associated with a greatly increased risk of heart attacks.

● Diabetic men have a two to three times greater risk of having a heart attack.
● Diabetic women have a five to six times greater risk of having a heart attack.
● Well controlled diabetics have a lower incidence of heart attacks than badly controlled diabetics.

There are two forms of diabetes:

● **Juvenile onset diabetes.** This form of diabetes may be inherited, and may come on spontaneously, although it is known to occur after an accident or virus infection. It usually starts in the early teens, and is almost always treated with injections of insulin as well as diet. Regrettably, there does not appear to be any way of preventing or curing this form of diabetes.

● **Mature onset diabetes.** This usually commences in middle to old age, and is strongly associated with obesity. However, recent evidence suggests that physical inactivity may be as important as the obesity in causing the diabetes. When the excess weight is lost the diabetic tendency often disappears. Mature onset diabetics are usually treated with diet, or diet supplemented by drugs. These drugs either change sugar metabolism, or increase insulin production by the pancreas.

The symptoms of diabetes are weight loss, excessive thirst, passing an excessive volume of urine, frequent infection, malaise and fatigue, abdominal pain and even coma. If you suspect that you may have diabetes, take a sample of urine (collected after a meal) to your GP who will test it for sugar.

Diabetes causes damage by blocking arteries and raising blood pressure and blood fats. The diabetic diet limits the amount of carbohydrates taken daily. The following foods are usually restricted:

● Biscuits and cakes
● Chocolates, sweets and pastries
● Sugar, honey and jam
● Bread, flour and potatoes
● Sweet and dried fruits
● Sauces and gravies.

It is very important for diabetics to control their diabetes by keeping strictly to their diet and medication, attending their doctor for regular medical check-ups, and frequently testing their blood or urine to measure the sugar level. All diabetics should carry an 'SOS Alert' bracelet or necklace stating that they are diabetic, and giving their current medication. This helps hospital doctors enormously in case of collapse and unconsciousness.

Excessive alcohol intake
Excessive alcohol intake is a risk factor for heart attacks. It is likely that taking 1-2 units of alcohol per day (1 unit = ½ pint of normal strength beer or lager, 1 glass of sherry or wine, 1 single measure of spirits) may slightly *reduce* a risk of a heart attack, but heavier drinking is associated with increased smoking, raised blood pressure, raised blood fats, obesity, lack of physical exercise, increased coffee intake, type A behaviour and stress, and consequently a much greater risk of a heart attack.

Women are more vulnerable to damage from alcohol. First, they have smaller livers and a lower capacity to remove alcohol from the blood. Secondly, they have a lower water content in their body (men 55-65% water, women 45-55% water), and since the alcohol remains in the water part of the body, the effective concentration and toxicity in women is higher for the same dose of alcohol.

Excessive intake of alcohol is strongly associated with many other diseases, including cirrhosis of the liver, inflammation of the stomach, several cancers, diabetes, epilepsy, brain failure and psychiatric problems. In addition, it is calculated that one in seven hospital admissions is for an alcohol-related disease, and the majority of road traffic accidents, many relationship problems and much personal violence is due to alcohol.

You should consider reducing or giving up alcohol if you

- drink more than 21 units a week (male), 14 units a week (female)
- drink more than twice a day or four times a week
- have one of the above diseases or problems
- take a drug that interacts with alcohol, for example tranquillisers, antidepressants, pain killers
- hope to start a family (male or female)
- are pregnant.

A reasonable target for alcohol intake, if it is equally spread over the week, is a maximum 14 units per week for men and 10 units per week for women.

If you feel that you drink too much, here are some strategies that will probably help you:

- Try to decide why you drink too much. Is it due to emotion, for example tension, anger, frustration, depression or happiness? Then deal with the underlying problem.

- Decide where you drink too much, and change your routine to avoid these places.

- Change your social life, and avoid your previous drinking partner(s). Examine your drinking pattern: see if you drink regularly every day, or just binge occasionally. Try to reduce the number of times you drink and the overall amount.

- Admit to yourself that you drink too much alcohol (or even that you are an alcoholic), and decide that you definitely want to give up completely (the best strategy). Failing that, decide to reduce your intake to a safe level.

- If you do find yourself in a pub, try a non-alcoholic drink, or else change to a different lower-alcoholic strength drink. Don't buy rounds, and reduce the volume by drinking half measures.

- Have an excuse ready to explain why you are not drinking, for example, 'I'm driving home, I'm saving money/losing weight, going out to dinner afterwards, had too much drink last night, on the wagon, doctor's orders.'

- Get expert help from your GP, or consult Alcoholics Anonymous — the local telephone number is in your phone book.

Gout

Heart attacks are more common in gout sufferers, who are also more likely to be obese and have raised blood pressure. The underlying problem in gout is a raised blood level of a substance called **uric acid.** This problem can either be inherited, or else caused by certain tablets (diuretics or aspirin) or diseases (leukaemias, psoriasis, renal failure). Gout is 25 times more common in men, and rarely occurs in women before the menopause.

The symptoms of gout are an exceptionally painful arthritis, especially in the big toe joint, and it is most likely to come on after one of the precipitating factors given below:

- Obesity and excess food intake (especially liver, kidney, offal, meat extracts and gravies, fish roe, anchovies and sardines).
- Starvation, due to breakdown of proteins while fasting.
- Alcohol, especially red wines, port, burgundy and also beer and shandy.
- Hot weather, low fluid intake and excess sweating (for example, mowing the lawn on a hot day).
- Exertion and exercise (for example, mowing the lawn on a hot day).
- Tissue damage and operations. ˙
- Stress and fatigue.

Generally speaking, if you do not have the family tendency to gout you will be rather unlucky to develop it. If you find that you have gout, you will probably be able to control it by losing weight, restricting the food mentioned in the list above, avoiding red fortified wines and making sure you drink plenty (4 pints of water a day, especially if the weather is hot and if you have been sweating or exerting yourself). If these measures fail to control the gout, then it may be necessary to take medicines as prescribed by your doctor.

Soft water
Extensive surveys around the world have associated soft water with a higher incidence of heart attacks. The reason for this is unknown, but certainly in Britain it may be due to the fact that people of the higher social classes I and II (professional and managerial) live in more affluent areas which tend to have hard water, whereas those of social classes IV and V (semiskilled and unskilled) live in industrial areas which tend to have soft water. The latter groups tend to have a much higher incidence of heart attacks and part of the problem may well be due to the soft water.

One suggestion for the difference is that the high level of calcium and magnesium in hard water in some way protects the heart. Other suggestions include the fact that soft water may contain a higher level of sodium and also of cadmium and lead. The latter is more likely if the domestic plumbing is still made of lead piping.

Heart disease and vitamins
The importance of vitamins has still not been fully evaluated, but it is possible that certain vitamins may be able to reduce the risk of heart attacks:

- **Vitamin C:** This helps the body fight stress, and detoxifies pollutants. It is particularly of value to smokers.
- **Vitamin E:** There is evidence that this may reduce blood clotting and increase transportation of oxygen in the blood.

SUMMARY

- There are many health consequences of being overweight, including an increased incidence of heart attacks.

- To lose weight you must change your eating habits for life and count calories. Your calorie intake must be less than your energy expenditure.

- When dieting, take three small meals a day and aim to lose one to two pounds a week.

- Mature onset diabetes can often be avoided by controlling obesity and taking regular exercise.

- Moderate your alcohol intake, and you will avoid many diseases including heart attacks.

- Gout is a risk factor for heart attacks, but can often be controlled by diet alone.

- Hard water appears to protect against heart attacks.

9
How to Reduce Stress

STRESS — THE UNDERRATED RISK FACTOR

By far the most underrated factor causing heart attacks is **stress.** There are many reasons for stress being so poorly appreciated as a risk factor but they include:

- Stress is usually more dependent upon a person's response to a situation rather than the situation itself. For example, a television appearance that brought blind panic to one individual might be welcomed in a calm and relaxed manner by another. Thus stress is not so much due to the *situation* but the *response* to that situation.

- The problem with stress is not merely the *amount* but also its *quality*: there is *good stress* (stimulation or fulfilment), and *bad stress* (anger or frustration), and it appears that the latter is far more likely to cause a heart attack, whereas the former may actually protect against one. For example, being the Prime Minister of Britain is an exceptionally responsible and stressful position, but no incumbent has suffered a heart attack whilst in office, because he (or she) is riding high on a wave of good stress through being successful enough to become and remain Prime Minister.

● There is, as yet, no objective way of measuring stress similar to measuring the number of cigarettes smoked, or blood pressure level or level of cholesterol. The usual observer of stress in the medical context will be a doctor, who is himself a member of a profession notorious for its highly stressful working conditions. Doctors often work 60-80 hours per week and take on enormous mental and emotional loads (with consequent high alcoholism and suicide rates). In the same way as an alcoholic is someone who drinks more than his doctor, 'a highly stressed ' person is someone who is under a greater stress than his doctor . . . and there are relatively few such people. Consequently the condition is greatly underdiagnosed.

Stress and heart attacks

Heart attack victims, prior to their attack, frequently suffer from frustration and depression, and demonstrate anxiety and nervousness when under stress. They may also experience an abnormal and deepening fatigue not refreshed by sleep, and, although working long hours (60 hours plus), little is achieved. They may have several jobs, but their work is surrounded with insecurity and feelings of being inadequate and unable to cope.

Often they will have suffered from some abrupt change or major event in their life (see long-term stress below) within three to six months before their attack. The greater this change and the shorter the interval before the attack, then the greater the incidence of sudden death.

STRESS — THE WESTERN DISEASE

Stress is in particular a western disease caused by an increasingly complex society. The pace of life is high, involving competitiveness from the cradle to the grave for recognition and rewards of all types, including money, possessions and a mate. Heart attacks are much less common in Japan, where the social structure, organised religion and extended family make up a far better support system than we have, for example, in Britain.

For many people in the western world, there is an increasing gap between their real personality and the person they are expected to be. Eventually, some find it too difficult to sustain the image of the person they are supposed to be and lapse into an illness, which is frequently a heart attack. Stress can be classified into:

- *Short-term stress.* This is caused by hour to hour events, and is easier to appreciate. It can be best analysed by keeping a 'stress diary' (see p.103). To reduce this sort of stress a precise definition of objectives is necessary in order to make the best use of time and resources.

- *Long-term stress.* This is caused by major events in life. It is well known that obviously negative events, like the death of a close friend or spouse, divorce or separation, going to jail, trouble with the police, accident or injury, financial or legal problems, unemployment or redundancy, are all stressful. However, apparently positive events, like marriage, job promotion and rise in salary, moving to a new house, pregnancy, retirement, changing schools, and holidays are also stressful. As a general rule the more changes that you have in your life in any one year, the more stressed you will become, and more likely to get ill.

With either short-term or long-term stress, it can frequently be a relatively minor event that causes the final collapse ('the straw that breaks the camel's back') and causes the heart attack.

Sources of stress in western society
Once again the important point to remember is that stress arises not so much from the situation, but the person's response to that situation.

- **Common stress provoking situations at work:** overwork (especially over 50 hours a week), more than one job, financial problems, too much or too little responsibility, problems with colleagues, subordinates and bosses, too much pressure and repeated deadlines, periods of unemployment or threatened redundancy, lack of recognition or support, frustrating work practices, night shifts, relocation and travel problems, legal problems.

- **Common stress problems at home:** prolonged marital disharmony, family disagreement, housing problems, lack of space and privacy, illness and death of relatives, looking after children and relatives, financial problems, legal problems.

Personality and stress
It has been found that heart attacks are more common amongst that certain type of personality American research has arbitrarily labelled Type A.

TCH—G

Type A personality

Type A personality is the fist-clenching, desk-banging executive type, constantly fighting to achieve more and more in less and less time. These personalities, usually men, have a very high drive towards often poorly-defined goals with consequent free 'floating anxiety'. They have 'hurry sickness' and a great eagerness to compete and be recognised. Their refusal to acknowledge tiredness or fatigue makes them liable to serious disease — including heart attacks.

Characteristically Type A personalities are very impatient, refuse to queue, and walk, talk and eat at the double. They tend to live life in the fast lane, and smoke, drink and eat too much. On average they have a higher blood pressure and cholesterol level, with a consequently far higher incidence of premature heart attacks and death.

Type B personality

Type B personalities are far more relaxed and passive, and are aware of their own limitations. They are rewarded for their temperate personalities by infrequently having heart attacks before retirement age.

Twentieth century 'stress circles'

Heart attacks were relatively uncommon before the 1930s in Britain. An important reason for this lower rate was that the level of stress was less, and the population exercised considerably more, due to the lack of labour-saving devices and motorised transport.

The diagrams on pp.100 and 101 give a rough quantitative comparison between the sources of stress, total stress and amount of reserve for a couple in the early twentieth century and a couple in the late twentieth century. It will be noticed that the sources of stress under each heading have altered due to changes in society. The size of reserve is the amount left after the rest of the circle has been filled.

Unlike the first couple, the couple in the late twentieth century stress circles are good candidates for heart attacks: they are under great stress and their reserve, which allows them to cope with further stress, is small — there is very little left to deal with an unexpected crisis.

The middle management pyramid

The picture on the next page summarises the position that middle management are frequently put in, sandwiched between the upper part of the pyramid composed of directors issuing unreasonable directives, and a base beneath comprising the shop floor making unreasonable demands for the available resources. The middle manager's job is thus often to try to reconcile the irreconcilable, usually at the expense of his or her own health.

THE MIDDLE MANAGEMENT PYRAMID

However, the situation in relation to heart attacks is now changing. Whereas in the 1950s and 1960s heart attacks may have been more common amongst executives and the professional classes in the boardrooms and amongst the middle managers, the highest incidence of heart attacks in the 1980s is amongst people lower down the pyramid, often in stressful, monotonous, boring jobs. It appears that those with higher incomes and better education (social classes I and II) now modify their behaviour and stop smoking, control their blood pressure, improve their diet and take regular exercise, thus reducing the likelihood of a heart attack. It is the semi-skilled and unskilled workers (social classes IV and V) on the shop floor, who have not modified their lifestyle, who now have the highest incidence of heart attacks.

HOW THE BODY REACTS TO STRESS

When the body finds itself in a stressful situation it reacts by releasing adrenalin and cortisol. These have the effect of raising the pulse, blood pressure and respiration rate, tensing the muscles and causing a dry mouth, dilating the pupils, and increasing the keenness of sight, hearing and concentration. The blood levels of sugar, fats and clotting factors are raised and digestion is stopped. All this is a very important survival mechanism and has saved many a person in a situation where

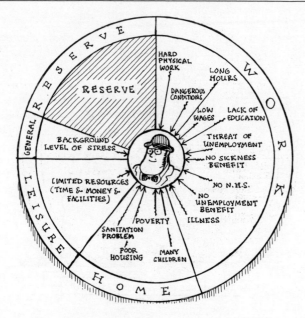

The early twentieth century 'stress circle' (male)

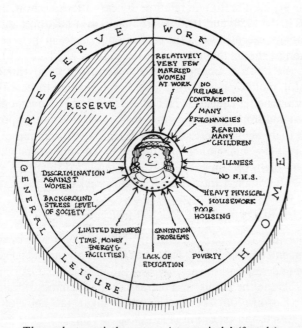

The early twentieth century 'stress circle' (female)

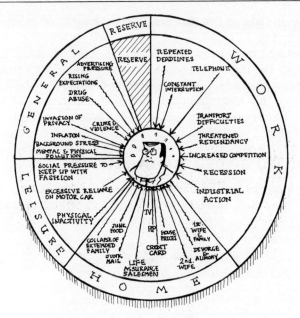

The late twentieth century 'stress circle' (male)

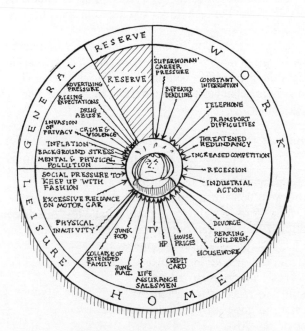

The late twentieth century 'stress circle' (female)

they have to fight or flee (for example, running from an unexpected bull in a field).

The damage from stress arises when this state of arousal becomes permanent. The fight or flight state is a very high output state which cannot be maintained for long. Constantly stressing a person and keeping them in this highly aroused state is the equivalent of taking a racehorse running the Derby at Epsom and asking it to continue at the same speed to John O'Groats.

HOW TO TELL IF YOU ARE UNDER STRESS

For short-term events the amount of stress is best assessed by keeping a 'stress diary' as shown on p.103. Assess your stress level as follows:

Stress level: 1 = slight stress
                 2 = moderate stress
                 3 = great stress
                 4 = very great stress

Quality of stress: + = stimulation or fulfilment
                    − = anger or frustration

Once you have identified the high stress point of your day, you will then be able to use the techniques suggested later to help you reduce and cope with stress.

For long-term stress, you will need to look at the number of changes that have occurred in your life in the past year. The greater the number of changes the greater the likelihood of serious disease. Try to avoid too many major changes to your lifestyle in any one year, especially as you get older.

Symptoms of stress
To tell if you are stressed look for the following symptoms:

- A frequent feeling of frustration or anger
- Inability to concentrate or make simple decisions
- A feeling of anxiety and/or depression and loss of self-confidence
- Irrational fear or even outright panic
- An increase or reduction in appetite
- Difficulty in getting to sleep or waking too early
- Weakness, tiredness or lethargy
- Inability to relax or to switch off
- Inability to cope with or finish jobs
- Loss of sex drive
- Fear of disease or death.

Stress Diary		Day	Date	
Time	Activity		Stress level (Rate 1-4)	Quality of stress (+ or −)
0-7 am				
7 am				
8 am				
9 am				
10 am				
11 am				
Noon				
1 pm				
2 pm				
3 pm				
4 pm				
5 pm				
6 pm				
7 pm				
8 pm				
9 pm				
10 pm				
11 pm				
m'night				

Changes in behaviour caused by stress:

- Irrational behaviour
- Increase in smoking
- Increased intake of medicinal drugs
- Increase in alcohol intake
- Uncharacteristic aggression or Type A behaviour
- Excess hand or teeth clenching
- Explosive mannerisms
- Reckless driving
- Increased or decreased sleep
- Memory or concentration impairment.

HOW TO HANDLE STRESS

In order to handle stress, you must fully understand what stress is (see descriptions of symptoms and behavioural effects of stress). Many people are unwittingly walking around with ideal recipes for stress inside their heads because they:

- are constantly working towards poorly defined objectives, and consequently have no means of telling if and when they have achieved the vague task that they have set themselves. For example, suppose you have said to yourself 'I want to be successful' — what does successful mean? a large house (how large?), a big car (is a Rolls Royce big enough?), an exotic holiday (is the Bahamas OK?)

- have totally impracticable and unreasonable expectations:

$$\text{Level of Stress} = \frac{\text{Expectations}}{\text{Achievements}}$$

High stress occurs when the expectations are far greater than the achievements.

In order to escape the effects of stress, especially bad stress (anger and frustration),

- analyse your present life, identify short-term and long-term stress and decide how much stress you will tolerate.
- remove as many sources of stress as possible.
- change your response to stress, ie don't just become cross, do something constructive like changing your job, leisure habits and outlook.
- use relaxation techniques to cope with stress.

How to remove sources of stress

- Decide your *real* objectives (probably very few). This is not easy since most people are conditioned to work on what is in front of them, rather than on defining the real problem and then solving that. Many problems are merely in your own and other people's heads.
- Sort activities into priority and do important things first.
- Plan realistically and set sensible deadlines for the available resources of time, energy and money.
- Concentrate completely on, and enjoy doing, one thing at a time.
- Ensure that your life is balanced. Have enough time for family and friends, exercise, hobbies and free unfilled time.
- Don't try to do everything yourself. Enlist the support of others at home and at work. Discuss the problem, communicate difficulties, set time limits and review progress regularly. Then let the other person get on with it, and don't be over critical.
- Know your own limitations — don't try to be superman or superwoman.
- Learn from your mistakes and the mistakes of others before they become your own.
- Give yourself regular holidays, adequate breaks at meal times and sufficient sleep.
- Anticipate and avoid stressful situations.
- Do your best, but if you do fail don't worry too much — and don't take yourself too seriously.

Change your response to stress

- Learn to assert yourself whilst still remaining sensitive and sympathetic. Don't become angry and aggressive, but instead confidently but coolly insist on having your point of view considered.
- Don't react 100% for small grievances or continue to grumble about old sources of annoyance.
- Analyse your behaviour, and don't become stressed when you feel uncomfortable, awkward, frustrated or dependent. Instead, try to find some other way to deal with your strong but negative feelings.
- Accept life as it is, warts and all. Accept that the Emperor has no clothes on, and don't get angry about it, because he isn't.

Techniques to help you cope with stress

- A strong relationship with another person is a very important factor in reducing the level and effect of stress. Being a member of an organisation, group or church is also beneficial in terms of stress management.

- Use natural relaxation techniques, and make them an integral part of your day (two twenty-minute sessions), together with exercise and vitamins. See relaxation as part of your exercise programe. Try breathing exercises and consider taking up structured relaxation techniques like yoga, meditation and self-hypnosis (these techniques are discussed in greater length in Chapter 10). All these techniques require 100% commitment and you can't do them with one eye on the clock, or when you are likely to be disturbed by the phone. Set aside a time and space that cannot be encroached upon by other activities or people. These relaxation techniques are then able to reverse the adverse effects of stress.

- Avoid 'instant' twentieth-century remedies to reduce stress such as tranquillisers, TV, cigarettes and alcohol. There are no short cuts.

SUMMARY

- The most underrated factor causing heart attacks is stress.

- Stress is caused not so much by the situation but the response to the situation.

- The most damaging stress is 'bad' stress (anger or frustration), whereas 'good' stress (stimulation or fulfilment), may actually be protective against heart attacks.

- To avoid stress, you must have realistic plans and expectations.

- To handle stress you must change your negative responses to situations and people.

10
How to Exercise and Relax

If stress is the most underrated risk factor for heart attacks, then the most underrated potential cure is physical exercise, supplemented with mental relaxation. Heart attacks were rare in the first quarter of the twentieth-century, when industrialisation and mechanisation was relatively new, and most activity proceeded at the speed of a trotting horse. Domestic electricity supply was almost unknown and most jobs at home were carried out by hand. Transport for the vast majority of people was on foot or bicycle.

Motorised transport started to become much more common in the 1930s and 1940s, as did labour-saving electrical devices. After a lag of 10-20 years (during which time the level of physical activity fell), heart disease started to rise dramatically. The reason for this enormous rise in heart disease has never been adequately explained, but the two risk factors that have risen most quickly have been stress and inactivity, whose ill effects have not been fully appreciated.

MORE EXERCISE, FEWER HEART ATTACKS

Evidence suggests that exercise reduces your risk of suffering a heart attack. An elegant study carried out in the 1950s compared heart attack rates in London for bus conductors and drivers (thus avoiding differences relating to socio-economic grouping, diet and living conditions). The study found that conductors had one quarter to one half the rate of heart attacks of the drivers, the conclusion being that the former were protected by the exercise of running up and down the stairs. In contrast the drivers, who were on average 15 lb heavier, remained immobile in their cabs.

In addition, a survey of San Francisco longshore men (dockers) found that those with a work pattern of repeated bouts of very vigorous exertion had one seventh of the rate of heart attacks when compared to longshore men with less vigorous work patterns.

Closer to home, a recent and extensive examination of the habits of a large number of British civil servants found that those who took regular vigorous exercise had one third the rate of heart attacks of those who took none.

Finally, it has been found that if you work at a desk, you are twice as likely to suffer a heart attack, compared to those who have more active occupations.

HOW EXERCISE HELPS YOUR BODY

Exercise seems to help by neutralising and reversing the biochemical and other changes associated with stress. Stress causes a rise in blood adrenalin level, with a secondary rise in pulse rate, blood pressure, blood sugar and fat levels and clotting factors.

After exercise all these levels are reduced, and the tissues and blood vessels are cleared of waste products. The resistance of the small arteries decreases, and the blood flows around the body more easily. You feel happier and sleep is much more refreshing.

In contrast, lack of exercise encourages raised blood pressure, raised blood fat levels, obesity, arthritis, thrombosis and depression.

EXERCISE AND THE TWENTIETH CENTURY

The evidence so far makes an overwhelming case in favour of exercise . . . However, modern twentieth-century lifestyles actually make it quite difficult to exercise. Insufficient attention and resources are devoted to helping people to make exercise an integral part of their lives.

Britain needs many more public sports facilities and sports teachers, and much more encouragement for adults to continue physical activity after leaving school. One way to help this would be to offer tax incentives to companies making sports facilities and teachers available to their workforce. This would stop exercise for adults being seen as a television spectator sport.

YOUR PERSONAL FITNESS PLAN

Your personal fitness plan should provide adequate physical exercise and mental relaxation. It will do this in three ways:

● By identifying changes that you can make in your lifestyle so that you are able to increase the exercise content of your day with only a little extra effort;
● By helping you to plan a thirty minute vigorous exercise session two to three times a week at an activity you enjoy;
● By introducing you to a relaxation technique.

A personal fitness plan is not a new idea, and in fact it was quite usual for the ancient Greeks to consult both a physician and a trainer in order to recover from illness. The former would diagnose and treat ailments, and the latter would work out a customised series of exercises and activities to get the patient back to fitness and health.

The body is a supply and demand machine, and if you don't use part of it, for instance a muscle, then it shrinks in size and becomes weak. Conversely, if you use a muscle, whether it be your biceps or your heart, it becomes stronger and works more efficiently: the heart muscle, too, can be trained by exercise the same as any other muscle in the body.

INCREASE THE EXERCISE CONTENT OF YOUR DAY

To do this, you need to make exercise and fitness an integral part of each day. The following are a few suggestions:

- Don't ride when you can walk.
- Park your car, or get off the bus several stops before your destination, and walk the remaining distance.
- Change your route so you can walk or run through the park (in daylight) on the way to work.
- Use the stairs, not the lift. If it is a skyscraper, get out four floors before your destination and walk the last four floors (your colleagues will be very impressed). If you are feeling a little less energetic, go four floors above your destination and walk down: it is still exercise. Do the same when leaving.
- Don't do everything by telephone. Make a personal visit sometimes. The exercise and face-to-face contact will help you work more efficiently.
- Buy a bicycle to ride to work. However, don't ride it in smog-filled underpasses or in the rain or snow when cycling is often dangerous.
- Use exercise as a substitute for other things you are cutting out of your life, such as cigarettes, alcohol, food.
- Use exercise as part of your stress management programme.

YOUR EXERCISE PLAN

Before you start your exercise plan, if you are over 35 you should first *check with your doctor* that you have no underlying health problems, especially heart disease. Then you need to (re)find an activity that you enjoy(ed) doing, and plan *gradually* to build up to exercising vigorously two to three times a week for twenty to thirty minutes a session. The idea whilst exercising is to raise your pulse to about 75% of the maximum safe pulse rate for your age. *Don't allow your pulse to go above this maximum safe rate.*

These two rates can be worked out from the formulae below:

Ideal exercising pulse rate per minute = 190 minus your age in years
Maximum safe pulse rate per minute = 220 minus your age in years

For example, if you are aged 50 years:

Ideal exercising pulse rate per minute   = 190 − 50 = 140
Maximum safe pulse rate per minute = 220 − 50 = 170

You should try to pick a **repetitive, isotonic, aerobic exercise** like swimming, running, jogging, dancing, one of the martial arts, tennis, cycling or a game involving running. Avoid an **isometric** exercise like weightlifting, horseriding or water skiing where there is little movement but more straining.

Before you start the exercise, have a 10 minute warm up with a lot of stretching, and when you finish have a similar cool down period. Leave two hours after a meal before exercising. Plan your exercise programme in advance, and don't put it at the end of the day when you are exhausted. Don't exercise whilst you are ill.

RELAXATION TECHNIQUES

These are excellent supplements to physical exercise, and stress management techniques as outlined in Chapter 9.

Breathing techniques
It is true to say that everyone who is alive knows how to breathe . . . or they are soon promoted to another category. However, enormous

benefit can be obtained from learning special **diaphragmatic breathing techniques.** These breathing techniques influence that part of the nervous system which is responsible for the secretion of adrenalin (the autonomic nervous system), and cause it to be set at a lower level. This helps relaxation and improves mood and sleep.

This breathing technique is best carried out lying flat on a blanket in a warm, quiet, dark room without interruptions. Make sure you are comfortable and close your eyes. Then take a deep breath — starting at your diaphragm fill the bottom of your chest, then fill the middle of your chest, and finally fill the top of your chest. You will probably be surprised at how much extra air you can take in.

After a moment's pause, steadily, at your own rate, start to breathe out, emptying first the bottom of your chest, then the middle of your chest, and finally the top of your chest.

Whilst you are doing this, you can also relax your whole body bit by bit, starting at your feet and moving up the body three inches at a time. Relax each three-inch segment as you breathe out. Feel yourself sinking into the floor with each exhalation and notice how, as each part becomes relaxed, it becomes as heavy as lead.

Eventually, the body will feel totally relaxed, and at this point you may even go off to sleep. When you have finished your relaxation session, start to move your fingers and toes gently, stretch your arms and legs, and slowly sit up.

This breathing and relaxation should be practised twice a day, taking about 20 minutes for each session.

Meditation and creative visualisation
Whilst you are in a deeply relaxed state induced by breathing or other methods, you can concentrate your mind completely on one image or thought. This may be a flower or other beautiful object, or even the suggestion that you will be successful with a particular project. This technique causes further relaxation and improves mood, confidence and energy level by a form of self-hypnosis.

Biofeedback
This technique is particularly popular on the West Coast of the USA. It is based on the finding that, when the body is particularly relaxed, pulse, blood pressure, respiratory rate, muscle tension and sweating are all reduced. Also, if the electrical activity of the brain is analysed, most brain waves are at or about eight cycles a second (the **alpha wave**).

All the variables mentioned above are controlled by the **autonomic nervous system.** This works without conscious effort — the individual is not aware of the level at which his or her autonomic system is set.

The basis of biofeedback is a machine which tells you how relaxed you are. The machine measures some variable controlled by the autonomic system, eg pulse, blood pressure, muscle tension, skin resistance or brain waves. Various relaxation techniques are then tried while you are connected to the machine to find a technique (breathing, meditation, creative visualisation) that particularly suits and relaxes you. Then you keep practising with this technique until you are able to go into a trance-like state and lower your own pulse, blood pressure and respiration rate.

The ideal way to learn any of the above techniques is from a qualified and experienced teacher. Addresses of teaching organisations are given in the appendix. The head office will be able to put you in touch with a local group, for whichever activity you choose.

SUMMARY

- Vigorous physical exercise prevents heart attacks by reducing blood pressure, blood fat levels, obesity and the effects of stress. It may also be used as a part of a 'Stop Smoking Programme'.

- Work out a personal fitness plan to increase the exercise content of your day, and arrange two or three thirty minute vigorous exercise sessions per week.

- Use relaxation techniques in conjunction with your physical exercise.

- More resources need to be made availale to encourage physical exercise in Britain.

11
How to Recover from a Heart Attack and Prevent a Recurrence

If you are unfortunate enough to have suffered a heart attack, this chapter will tell you how to adjust, and reduce your risk of sustaining another one. The first part of the chapter takes up the story after your discharge from hospital, and the second part deals with possible complications with their further investigation and treatment.

EFFECTS OF A HEART ATTACK

A heart attack is almost always an unexpected event, even in a person with many strong risk factors. The full physical, and especially mental, effects often do not show until weeks after discharge from hospital. These include alternating feelings, on the one hand, of anger, rage, denial and panic and, on the other hand, of vulnerability, helplessness, resignation, depression and despair. Many patients have few sources of mental, emotional and spiritual support with which to sustain themselves because of the modern tendency towards looser family ties and lack of community involvement in an organised religion or belief system.

CORONARY AFTERCARE

There are two views on coronary aftercare:

● The first is that the heart attack should be seen as an unfortunate incident; the patient has now, fortunately, recovered and the sooner he or she gets on with living life the same as before the better. There will be just a few small inconveniences like taking a few pills and stopping smoking.
● The second view, which this book favours, is that if you have suffered a heart attack your lifestyle is not correct for your body, and to prevent a further attack you must in some way alter that lifestyle.

TCH—H

Convalescence and retraining

In order to have a chance of full recovery, a heart attack patient needs an extended period of convalescence and retraining. This period allows the patient to get over the exhaustion and often near terminal stress that caused the heart attack in the first place. Time is also needed to cope with the strong emotions described above.

When the patient is no longer mentally and physically exhausted, he or she is then in a position to work out a rational plan to reduce the level of risk factors. After discussing plans and possibilities with his or her partner and family, the patient may decide on a major lifestyle change, perhaps including a re-evaluation and re-adjustment of job, financial status and housing.

These changes are, of course, in themselves stressful, hence the need for plenty of rest. However, to use the analogy of a game of football, the first attack is the equivalent of being shown the yellow warning card, and the wise player makes sure that he doesn't repeat the offence and get sent off for an early shower.

During this period of recuperation too much stimulation from visitors or television watching is not advisable as this can be very exhausting. The patient should be reviewing all elements of his or her lifestyle to see how known risk factors can be reduced, for example stopping smoking, reducing blood pressure, reducing blood fat levels, losing weight, moderating alcohol intake, and taking more exercise.

Exercise

Your convalescence and recovery programme needs to be a balance between mental and physical rest, but you must also have sufficient stimulation to prevent you from becoming bored. It is important to increase exercise tolerance, but gradually. A reasonable objective is to start walking a little at the end of the first week after discharge from hospital. You should plan to go up and down steps only once a day and spend the rest of the time sitting in a chair. For the second week, providing the weather is not too cold, walking in the garden and house is a good objective. For the third week walking half a mile outside the house accompanied by another fit adult would probably be right. In the fourth week, the objective is to walk a mile or so a day. Sexual activity can be restarted gradually from the fourth week.

Return to work
Plan to return to work, subject to medical approval, after about two or three months, but only after you have sorted out underlying problems. If you have a heavy manual job it may be necessary to move to a lighter occupation, especially if you work at a height or in dangerous conditions. Certain jobs, mostly in the transport industry, cannot be continued after a heart attack. These include HGV and PSV drivers, engine drivers, airline pilots, air traffic controllers and divers.

Management of stress
Stress management is very important, and you will need to take certain strategies from your recuperation into your everyday life. These are designed to make your behaviour more like the B type personality and less like the A type (see p.98).

You should reduce your aggression and the number of objectives you are working on at any one time. Don't take on anything new without dropping an existing activity. Be more relaxed and listen to others more. Give yourself 100% to what you are doing at any particular moment, even if you are only brushing your teeth.

Avoid stressful situations, and viewing violent and competitive events such as TV news and sport. Do things more slowly, including walking, talking, eating and driving. Use waiting time (queueing, for instance) to reflect, and speak with your partner, family, neighbours and friends more.

Realise that the cause of stress is not so much the problem in front of you, but your *perception* of it. Don't see all events as a direct challenge to you.

Complications
There are a number of well recognised possible complications after discharge from hospital for a heart attack patient. These include:

- Angina
- Irregularities of the heart beat
- Chronic heart failure
- Blood clots.

ANGINA

This is a severe chest pain originating from the heart and is caused by insufficient blood supply to the heart muscle. It occurs as a result of a partial blockage of one or both of the coronary arteries.

The pain usually occurs in the centre of the chest and feels like a heavy weight or a tight band. It may radiate down the left arm or into the neck or jaw. The pain is not present at rest, but starts after exercise or exertion, especially in the cold. Anger, stress or emotion, smoking and large meals may also set off angina.

The intensity of the pain forces the patient to stop whatever he or she is doing, and then the pain disappears. It is also relieved by a glyceryl trinitrate tablet placed under the tongue.

However, if an angina attack lasts for more than twenty minutes, and is not relieved by a glyceryl trinitrate tablet **then a heart attack is likely to have occurred and medical attention should be sought immediately.**

The treatment of angina depends upon its severity. Initial measures like stopping smoking, reducing blood pressure, losing weight, avoiding stress and adopting an exercise programme may help, but if that fails then drugs may need to be tried. There are three groups.

Drugs for angina

Nitrates
Nitrates are suitable for all patients with angina. They work by dilating the coronary arteries (improving the blood supply to the heart muscle), and dilating blood vessels throughout the body (thus reducing the blood returning to the heart and the work done by the heart muscle). These drugs usually work very quickly (within 30 seconds), but their effect lasts for only a quarter of an hour. Long-acting preparations are also available which are taken only once or twice a day. They are directly absorbed from the mouth, which has a rich blood supply. Side effects include headaches, flushing and a feeling of faintness when standing up.

Beta-blockers
These may also be used for angina, especially in patients with raised blood pressure, fast heart rate and anxiety, although in susceptible in-

dividuals they can cause heart failure and asthma. They work by slowing the heart rate, reducing the strength of the contractions of the heart muscle, and lowering the blood pressure, with a consequent drop of oxygen consumption of the heart muscle.

Calcium antagonists
These work by increasing coronary blood flow, reducing blood pressure and lessening the strength of the contraction of the heart muscle. This effect is achieved by slowing the transfer of calcium across the heart muscle cell membrane.

Verapamil is also used to stop certain sorts of irregularity of heart beat, but must be given with care when used simultaneously with a beta-blocker.

Further investigation of angina
If the above measures and medicines do not relieve angina, then it may be necessary to undergo further investigations, and even surgery.

The first investigation is the **exercise ECG.** It is carried out either at about 2 weeks or 2 months after the heart attack, first at rest and then whilst the patient is riding a static bicycle or walking on a treadmill. If the patient's heart muscle is being starved of oxygen then it will show on the ECG.

If the angina is particularly severe it may be advisable to carry out a 'cardiac catheterisation', and an X-ray investigation of the heart. To do this a small thin tube is passed along the femoral artery in the thigh up to the heart and the pressures in the heart chambers can be measured (as shown in Fig. 9). X-ray opaque dye can be squirted along the

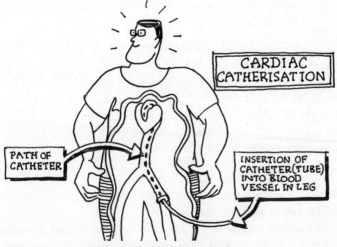

Fig. 9: Cardiac catherisation

catheter, thus showing up the outline of the heart, and also the outline of the coronary artery at the site of the blockage.

If the blockage is severe, then it may be advisable to clear it. This may be done by passing a balloon on the end of a catheter along the coronary artery. More usually a **coronary bypass graft** is performed (see p.12) in which a piece of vein is taken from the patient's leg and used to join the aorta and the coronary artery (on the far side of the blockage). This procedure cures 60% of angina cases, and gives relief to another 30%. However, there is a 1% mortality rate for the operation, and although the quality of life for the surviving 99% may be improved, the life expectancy is unchanged.

IRREGULARITIES OF THE HEART BEAT

About 90% of heart attack cases suffer from some sort of irregularity in the heart beat in the first few days. This is due to an electrical problem which affects the rate and rhythm of the heart beat.

When the heart beats irregularly, or too fast or too slowly, then the pumping action is usually inefficient; this may cause angina, palpitations, heart failure or fainting. An ECG is absolutely vital for diagnosis of these sorts of problems, hence the reason for continuous monitoring of heart patients in coronary care units.

Quite commonly these irregularities of the heart beat do not occur constantly, but are intermittent and last for only a few minutes of each day. The way to diagnose such rhythm disturbances is to give the patient a 24-hour ECG, which is recorded on a small cassette player worn continuously for one day.

Drugs are available that can speed the heart up, slow it down or prevent abnormal rhythms.

Pacemakers

If the heart's natural pacemaker mechanism is damaged, then the heart may beat much too slowly (at 30-40 beats per minute). This causes drowsiness and weakness at rest, and fainting on trying to move. The best answer is to insert an artificial electrical device, also called a **pacemaker,** to replace the heart's natural but failing one.

Pacemakers may be fitted externally on the skin over the heart for short-term use. Alternatively, for long-term use, an internal pacemaker may be inserted, either along the femoral or subclavian vein **(transvenous pacemaker)**, or sewn to the outside surface of the heart **(epicardial pacemaker)** — see Fig. 10.

The pacemaker weighs only 2-4 ounces, and the lithium batteries are able to last 5-10 years. The most usual sort of pacemaker used is a

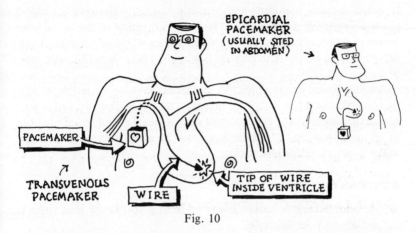

Fig. 10

'demand pacemaker', which only cuts in when the heart rate drops below a predetermined rate (eg 60 beats per minute). There are now also 'smart' pacemakers that can detect the circulating level of adrenalin and adjust the heart rate accordingly. There are even pacemakers that can detect that the heart has stopped and restart it.

CHRONIC HEART FAILURE

This is the long-term failure of the heart to pump an adequate amount of blood around the body. If it occurs soon after a heart attack there is often a secondary drop in blood pressure. The larger the size of the heart attack (the more muscle damage), the greater the risk of heart failure.

If heart failure happens soon after a heart attack, the patient may go into 'shock', rather similar to that caused by a haemorrhage. One of the commonest causes of heart failure is an irregularity of the heart beat. This is treated as described in the previous section.

The surgical treatment for heart failure, which cannot be treated by any other method, is a **heart transplant.** Although this has received a great deal of publicity, it is not very widely used. The problem is that there are often frequent complications due to rejection of the donor heart by the recipient. Ideal candidates (recipients) for heart transplant are under 40 years of age, and without any other serious illness, like infection, diabetes or malignant disease.

BLOOD CLOTS AND EMBOLI

Patients who have had a heart attack have an increased incidence of **blood clots** in the lungs, brain and legs. The blood clots are encouraged by many factors, including a poor cardiac output (allowing the blood to settle in veins), prolonged bed rest, concentration of the blood (due to use of diuretics), and an increased stickiness of blood platelets. Consequently, the best way to prevent blood clots is early mobilisation out of bed.

Anticoagulant drugs which thin the blood have been tried to prevent this complication but with little success. One of the few successful prophylactic measures for preventing a second heart attack is a daily dose of 75 mg of aspirin (a 'junior' aspirin). The aspirin seems to work by making the platelets less sticky.

SUMMARY

● A heart attack is nature's way of letting you know that there is a flaw in your lifestyle.

● To reduce the likelihood of a second heart attack, you must recuperate properly. Then before restarting work try to reduce all risk factors.

● If you have complications follow medical advice and take medication as prescribed.

12
General Practice Screening

Great Britain now has the dubious qualification of being the heart attack centre of the world. Unlike other countries, such as the USA, Australia and Finland, which have reduced their previously high heart attack rates, Britain now leads the field with 180,000 heart attack deaths per year. This is equivalent to wiping out the entire populations of the cities of York and Cheltenham annually.

In addition, there is a great financial loss to the country from heart disease, some 25 million working days being lost per year representing £1,100 million in lost production.

The best way to reduce heart attacks is not by better immediate care after the event but by previous attention to the known risk factors such as smoking, raised blood pressure and raised cholesterol level (see Chapter 2). If these risk factors are reduced enough at an early stage, then this will *prevent* the processes that cause heart attacks.

WHAT IS SCREENING?

This is a way of detecting diseases at an early stage (see the scale of health, Zones A and B, on p.36) before permanent changes have set in. Not all diseases are suitable for screening, but heart disease is one that can be reduced by a screening and education scheme.

To decide whether a disease is suitable for a screening programme there are certain criteria that should be fulfilled. It should be:

- common in the population screened
- dangerous if not treated
- treatable at an early stage without major side effects
- reasonably easy to find

and the patient/treatment organisation needs to have:

121

- adequate resources for treatment of the disease
- adequate resources for recall, review of treatment and repeat screening.

It is important, however, to note that 'if any preventative (or screening) measure is likely to expose many people to a small risk, then the harm is likely to outweigh the benefits' (Rose's Dictum, the theory of Dr Rose, an expert on screening procedures). Thus any large-scale screening programme must be virtually without risk to the patients screened.

WHY SCREEN FOR HEART DISEASE?

Screening is necessary for two reasons.

- Many of the risk factors are *symptomless;* there is no external sign, even to the patient, that he or she is suffering from raised blood pressure, raised cholesterol level or diabetes.

- Due to lack of *patient education* the full significance of many risk factors is underappreciated, for example obesity, family history of heart disease, lack of exercise, smoking, alcoholism and contraceptive medication. Consequently patients with these risk factors do not adjust their lifestyle to lower their overall risks.

SCREENING APPROACHES

There are three sorts of screening for heart disease:

- **Mass screening (mass strategy).** This sort of screening brings a large drop in the total number of deaths since the whole population is being treated. However, it is expensive, and the detection rate of high risk candidates is low. Rather than mass screening, a more appropriate national strategy to reduce heart attacks would probably be **mass education** via the media of television, radio, newspapers and magazines. This could be used to encourage the whole population to change their smoking, eating and exercise habits, learn to manage stress and get their blood pressure checked. It is probably by this mechanism that the heart attack rate has dropped 30-40% in the USA and Australia.

- **Selective screening (high risk strategy).** This is the screening of a small proportion of the population who have been pre-selected because of some factor — such as family history of a very high cholesterol level — that identifies them as highly likely to suffer a heart attack. This type of screening gives a big benefit but only for a small number of people since the underlying conditions are not that common.

- **Opportunistic screening.** This is a combination of the above two techniques, where people attending a doctor (usually a general practitioner) for some other condition are asked about their smoking, eating and drinking habits, and their blood pressure, height and weight measured. This will reveal high risk individuals (case finding) which can then be selectively screened in greater depth.

SCREENING IN BRITAIN

Unlike in the USA, where health checks (including full physical examinations, blood tests and exercise ECGs) are routine, before 1982 there was no large heart attack screening programme in the UK. Then the Oxford Prevention of Heart and Stroke Project was set up as an experiment, and this proved so successful that it has been continued and expanded all over Britain.

There are many reasons why screening for heart attacks had not been started before in Britain. These include:

- Apathy amongst the population who see little reason to be screened, since if they are ill there are relatively few adverse financial consequences: the NHS will pick up the bill for all necessary treatment. The situation in the USA is completely different, and a minor illness can be a large financial burden, whereas a major illness can even cause bankruptcy. Consequently, Americans are far more keen on staying healthy.

- A problem with the basic philosophy of the National Health Service, which is more orientated towards illness than health: a more appropriate title would be the National Sickness Service. The doctors in the NHS are very dedicated and have great expertise in terms of disease and its treatment . . . but little or no training in the promotion of *health*. So, often the doctors are put in a situation where they are confronted with a desperately ill patient whom they try valiantly (but often in vain) to cure. If the patient had been given adequate health education in advance they would be far less likely to become ill. To draw an analogy with another emergency service, it is rather like the fire brigade watching a child playing with matches, but not reacting until the house is burning down. A more appropriate, but less sensational action, would be merely to take the matches away from the child and educate it to the dangers of fire.

The Oxford Prevention of Heart and Stroke Project

In the Oxford Prevention of Heart and Stroke Project patients attending their GP for another reason were offered a free 'Human MOT' to be carried out by the practice nurse.

The screening was carried out at the GP's surgery on an opportunistic basis. It was already known that 70% of a GP's patients attend in any one year period, and 95% attend over a five year period. This fact was seen as an opportunity to offer all patients registered at that surgery a health check once every five years.

Usually screening procedures (cervical screening, for instance) depend on patients volunteering themselves for a check. Such tests tend to be far better taken up by social classes I and II, but neglected by social classes IV and V, who are the most likely to suffer from the diseases. The opportunistic screening programme was immediately very popular and there was a 90% uptake of appointments with a low rate of missed appointments.

The screening session

The screening was carried out by the practice nurse and took twenty minutes per patient. There was an emphasis on an informal, relaxed atmosphere, possibly more easily achieved by the nurse than the GP. The nurse took details of smoking, eating, drinking and exercise habits, medication and family history of angina, heart disease, strokes and diabetes. The patient was then measured for height, weight and blood pressure, the urine tested for sugar and protein, and blood cholesterol estimation arranged at the hospital.

The nurse then gave advice on how to adjust lifestyle, using leaflets where necessary on the subjects of diet, weight reduction (reducing salt, sugar and fat, and raising dietary fibre), stopping smoking and alcohol intake. She gave a target date for stopping smoking, weight loss or change of diet. Patients with raised blood pressure, raised blood fat levels or diabetes were referred to the GP for further assessment and treatment.

Other health counselling was also carried out where appropriate, and cervical smears, breast screening and tetanus injections were given as required.

Success of the Project

The findings of the Oxford group were that

- 75% of patients seen had at least one risk factor,
- 25% had two risk factors, and

● 10% had all three major risk factors (cigarette smoking, raised blood pressure and obesity/raised blood fat levels).

The Oxford Prevention of Heart and Stroke Project has already shown itself to be successful in causing a 12% drop in the incidence of heart attacks in the area:

    1985/1986: Weekly heart attack incidence 4.1 per 100,000
    1986/1987: Weekly heart attack incidence 3.6 per 100,000

A local initiative
In Solihull there has been particular interest in screening. The Solihull Family Practitioner Committee has sponsored the production of a 'Health Screening Passport' for heart attacks and strokes, which is linked to this book and written by the same author.

The Health Screening Passport is modelled on the British Government Passport. Colour coding is used throughout, both to highlight the risk factors and to indicate the various sections to be completed. Patients are given the Passport a few days before their screening appointments so that they can complete various sections themselves.

As patients are thus able to answer many of the routine questions in advance, more of the 20-minute appointment is available to advise them on ways to reduce their risk factors. Patients can more easily appreciate the value of screening: the Passport provides a 'snapshot' of their risk factors at first screening, and when they are later re-screened the beneficial effect of stopping smoking, changing diet, exercise habits, stress reduction is brought home to them by their improved figures. (See p.145 for details of how to obtain copies of the Passport.)

THE FUTURE OF SCREENING

Car owners in Britain expect to have their cars serviced every 6,000 or 10,000 miles. It is to be hoped that the population of Britain will come to expect to 'service' their bodies too (that is have them screened). You can change your car, but for the foreseeable future it will not be possible to change your body.

There is little doubt that the best place for opportunistic heart screening is in general practice, and the Oxford project has confirmed the value of screening in reducing heart attacks and promoting health. However, on a realistic note, it has to be mentioned that most GPs are already hard pushed treating their existing patients in the conventional way. For heart screening to be viable GPs need considerable extra resources to allow them to operate such schemes properly: a quality service cannot be offered on a shoestring.

SUMMARY

- Opportunistic heart screening at the level of the general practice can reduce the incidence of heart attack.

- Any national heart screening programme must be supplemented by long-term health education of the population via the mass media.

- The National Health Service needs to give a greater emphasis to the promotion of a healthy lifestyle.

- For general practice opportunistic screening to be successful, it must be adequately resourced.

13
How to Resuscitate an Unconscious Patient

This chapter will tell you how to resuscitate someone who has collapsed. It can be used by someone with no previous knowledge of cardiopulmonary resuscitation. Follow the instructions slowly and carefully and DON'T PANIC.

If you come across someone who has collapsed then you must answer the next three questions to decide if you need to use cardio-pulmonary resuscitation (CPR).

1. **Are they unconscious?**　　　Yes/No
   — Pinch them hard —
   if they don't react
   they are unconscious.

   If three yeses go straight to p.129 and start cardio-pulmonary resuscitation.

2. **Have they stopped breathing?**　　　Yes/No
   — Listen with your
   ear over their nose
   and mouth for air
   entering and leaving,
   and look for chest
   movements.

   If patient is merely unconscious and not breathing but the heart is beating go to p.131.

3. **Has their heart stopped beating?**　　　Yes/No
   — Feel for carotid or
   radial pulse or heart
   beat — see diagram
   on p.128. Compare with
   your own.

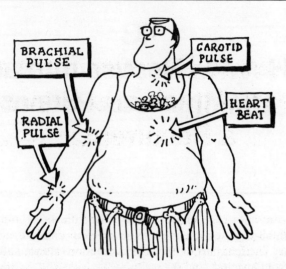

If the answer to any of these questions is no, then you are not deal-ing with a cardiac arrest — the heart has not stopped beating and cardio-pulmonary resuscitation is not necessary. The cause of the collapse will be some other reason — a faint, obstructed airway, epilepsy, alcoholic intoxication, diabetic coma (too much or too little sugar in the blood), overdose of tablets or narcotics, or hypothermia.

If the patient is not breathing then they must be given the kiss of life as shown on p.131. If they are merely unconscious, medical atten-tion and assessment is still needed but all that is necessary in the short term is to place the unconscious person on their left or right side coma position (see diagram) so that they do not inhale their own vomit if they are sick.

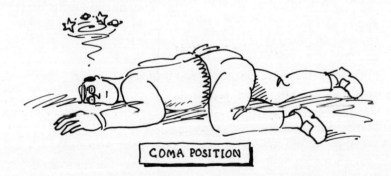

COMA POSITION

If your patient is unconscious, not breathing and without heart beat and if there are more than two of you, send one for medical assistance. Those remaining should immediately start cardio-pulmonary resuscitation. This can be carried out quite successfully by someone with no previous training. By carefully reading this chapter and following the instructions below, you will be able to carry out this life-saving technique. The object is to restart the heart beating, but failing that to send oxygenated blood to the brain, which will be severely and permanently damaged if it is starved of oxygenated blood for more than 4 minutes.

INSTRUCTIONS FOR CPR (CARDIO-PULMONARY RESUSCITATION)

NB: This must not be attempted if the heart is beating even faintly.

1. Make sure the patient is lying on a flat firm surface: the floor is usually the best place. A mattress is too soft unless boards are put underneath it.

2. Make sure that the patient's airway is clear of vomit and dentures — clear it with your finger if necessary.

3. Start cardio-pulmonary resuscitation. This consists of two parts, which have to be done alternately, since it is very difficult even for two people to do them simultaneously.

    (a) **External heart massage.** This is carried out by pressing firmly on the centre of the breast bone (sternum) with both hands, pushing it down between one and a half to two inches. This

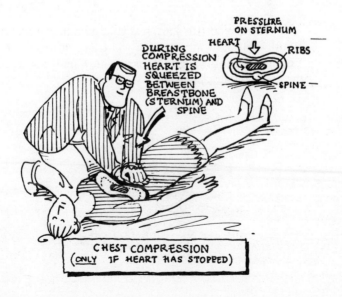

requires a lot of force, so use your body weight to do the work. You should be aiming at a rate just slightly faster than one push per second (saying 'ruff! ruff!, ruff! ruff!' will give you the rate). The squeezing of the chest wall will push the blood around the body to the brain and compensate for the heart not beating.

If there are two of you, do five heart pushes and then one ventilation of chest as in (b) below. If you are alone, do fifteen pushes on the heart then two chest ventilations as in (b).

(b) **Ventilation of chest.** This involves filling the patient's lungs with air of your own (there is still plenty of oxygen left for the patient to use). You should have already cleared the airway but you will need to tilt the patient's head back as far as it will go to open the throat.

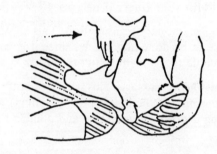

Squeeze the nostrils shut, seal your mouth over the patient's mouth, and blow air in which will travel down to the lungs. You should see the chest rise as you blow in; if not, check that the airway is not blocked.

If there are two operators, do one breath to five heart pushes. If you are on your own do two breaths to fifteen heart pushes.

Carry on alternating steps (a) and (b) until the patient recovers, or for thirty minutes. With two operators you may need to change over after a few minutes since the breathing out can make you dizzy.

If the heart starts beating, stop the chest pushes and continue breathing once every 3-4 seconds. As the patient recovers their colour will improve (from blue-black to pink), and their pupils will probably get smaller.

When the patient recovers put him/her into the coma position (see p.128). Make sure that the patient's heart does not stop beating and that he or she does not stop breathing until help arrives.

The 'kiss of life'
This technique is used if the patient is unconscious and not breathing, but the heart is beating. It is carried out as in (b) **Ventilation of the chest** above.

When help arrives
In hospital or even a cardiac ambulance there will be more facilities for resuscitation including:

- **Oxygen** with a means to get it into the lungs.
- **An ECG machine** — an essential diagnostic aid to find out the problem with the heart.
- **A defibrillator** — a machine to give the heart an electrical shock which makes all the heart muscles and fibres beat together rather than separately (fibrillation).
- **A drip or intravenous line** which allows appropriate drugs to be sent along the veins towards the heart and possibly restore the heart beat to normal.

Cardio-pulmonary resuscitation is widely taught in American cities, which may partly explain their lower mortality rate from heart attacks.

If CPR is started within one minute of a heart attack the chances of recovery are better than 95%. If CPR is delayed for four minutes, the chance of recovery is 15%. If there is a seven minute delay the victim has only an 8% chance of survival.

SUMMARY

- By reading this chapter you can learn cardio-pulmonary resuscitation, which may save someone's life.

- When you come across a collapsed person, look for unconsciousness, breathing and heart beat.

- To decide on the appropriate resuscitation technique check below:

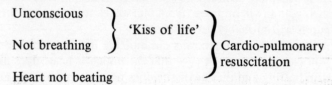

- Cardio-pulmonary resuscitation consists of two alternating procedures:

  (a) External cardio-massage — 5 beats at approximately 1 per second
  and
  (b) Ventilation of the chest — 1 breath every 5 cardiac massages.

14
Conclusions

This chapter is deliberately very brief, so as not to dilute its message.

CONCLUSIONS FOR THE INDIVIDUAL

● Heart attacks can be avoided by attention to the known risk factors.

● The major risk factors for heart attacks are smoking, raised blood pressure and raised blood fat levels.

● The minor risk factors are obesity, diabetes, lack of exercise, family tendency to heart attacks, stress, personality type, alcohol, oral contraceptive pill, gout and soft water.

● To avoid a heart attack, patients should attend a screening clinic and find the value of their risk factors. They should then, where necessary, modify their lifestyle to reduce their overall risk.

CONCLUSIONS FOR SOCIETY

Heart attacks may be reduced by attention to known risk factors. The following concrete proposals would reduce the heart attack risk of almost everyone in Britain:

● To reduce smoking, tobacco advertising and sponsorship of sporting events should be phased out over the next five years. Greater steps should be taken to avoid passive smoking in public places and at work.

● The food industry has a vital part to play in the prevention of heart disease by reducing the fat, sugar and salt content of food. It would be helpful if all packaged food was labelled with an analysis of protein, carbohydrates, fat, salt and calorie content.

● Britain requires many more sports facilities and sports teachers and much more encouragement for adults to continue physical activity after leaving school. One way to facilitate this change would be to offer preferential tax allowances to companies making sports facilities available for their workforce.

● Any national heart screening programme must be supplemented by long-term health education of the population via the mass media.

Conversion Table for Height

Feet and inches to centimetres (1″ = 2.54 cm)

Feet/Inches	Centimetres	Feet/Inches	Centimetres
4′ 6″	137.5	5′ 8″	172.5
4′ 7″	140	5′ 9″	175
4′ 8″	142.5	5′ 10″	177.5
4′ 9″	145	5′ 11″	180
4′ 10″	147.5	6′ 0″	182.5
4′ 11″	150	6′ 1″	185
5′ 0″	152.5	6′ 2″	187.5
5′ 1″	155	6′ 3″	190
5′ 2″	157.5	6′ 4″	192.5
5′ 3″	160	6′ 5″	195
5′ 4″	162.5	6′ 6″	197.5
5′ 5″	165	6′ 7″	200
5′ 6″	167.5	6′ 8″	202.5
5′ 7″	170	6′ 9″	205

Conversion Table for Weight

Stones and pounds to kilograms (1 kg = 2.2 lb)

st lb	kg	st lb	kg	st lb	kg
6 0	38.1	8 6	53.5	10 12	68.9
6 2	39.0	8 8	54.4	11 0	69.9
6 4	39.9	8 10	55.3	11 2	70.8
6 6	40.8	8 12	56.2	11 4	71.7
6 8	41.7	9 0	57.2	11 6	72.6
6 10	42.6	9 2	58.1	11 8	73.5
6 12	43.5	9 4	59.0	11 10	74.4
7 0	44.5	9 6	59.9	11 12	75.3
7 2	45.4	9 8	60.8	12 0	76.2
7 4	46.3	9 10	61.7	12 2	77.1
7 6	47.2	9 12	62.6	12 4	78.0
7 8	48.1	10 0	63.5	12 6	78.9
7 10	49.0	10 2	64.4	12 8	79.8
7 12	49.9	10 4	65.3	12 10	80.7
8 0	50.8	10 6	66.2	12 12	81.6
8 2	51.7	10 8	67.1	13 0	82.6
8 4	52.6	10 10	68.0	13 2	83.5

st lb	kg	st lb	kg	st lb	kg
13 4	84.4	15 8	98.9	17 12	113.4
13 6	85.3	15 10	99.8	18 0	114.3
13 8	86.2	15 12	100.7	18 2	115.2
13 10	87.1	16 0	101.6	18 4	116.1
13 12	88.0	16 2	102.5	18 6	117.0
14 0	88.9	16 4	103.4	18 8	117.9
14 2	89.8	16 6	104.3	18 10	118.8
14 4	90.7	16 8	105.2	18 12	119.7
14 6	91.6	16 10	106.1	19 0	120.7
14 8	92.5	16 12	107.0	19 2	121.6
14 10	93.4	17 0	107.9	19 4	122.5
14 12	94.3	17 2	108.9	19 6	123.4
15 0	95.2	17 4	109.8	19 8	124.3
15 2	96.2	17 6	110.7	19 10	125.2
15 4	97.0	17 8	111.6	19 12	126.1
15 6	98.0	17 10	112.5	20 0	127.0

Weight Loss Charts and Instructions

Instructions

Weigh yourself at the same time each day (eg before breakfast), preferably naked, but failing that without shoes and wearing the same amount of indoor clothes on each occasion. Using the charts on the following pages fill in your own starting weight at the solid horizontal line marked 0. Then make a graph of your weight loss by filling in the chart each day, moving down one unit for each pound lost (you may use kilograms if desired). There is a dot to represent each day of the week.

Remember four rules

1. Change your eating habits: plan to eat mostly low calorie foods.
2. Decide on a daily calorie allowance: it must be *less* than your daily calorie requirement to lose weight. Divide that calorie allowance into meal allowances (eg 1,000 calories a day divided into: breakfast 300 calories, lunch 350 calories, evening meal 250 calories, drinks and snacks 100 calories).
3. Take three small meals a day: don't fast all day and then take one large meal since even on a low calorie intake you will gain weight.
4. Have a realistic weight loss target: one to two pounds a week.

Weight Loss Chart

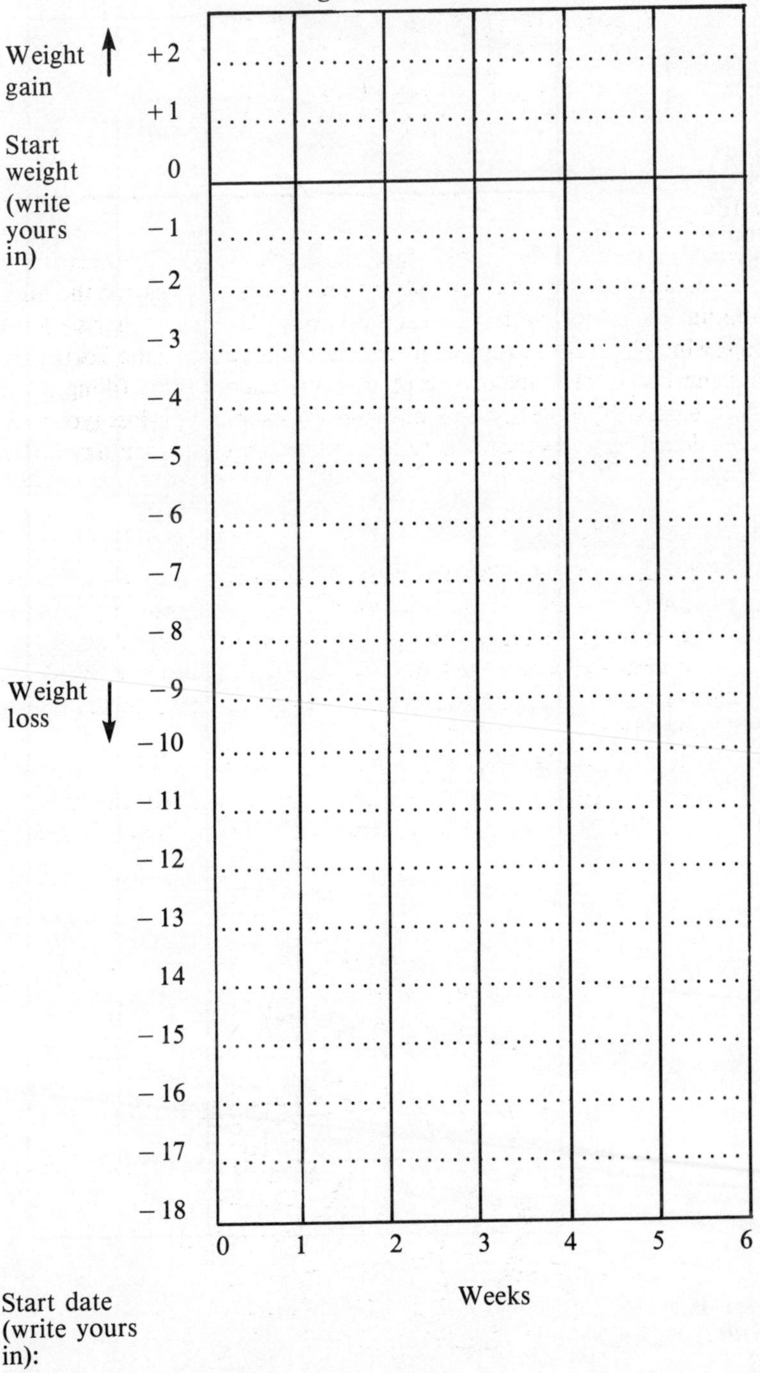

Weight gain ↑ +2
+1

Start weight (write yours in) 0

−1
−2
−3
−4
−5
−6
−7
−8

Weight loss ↓ −9
−10
−11
−12
−13
14
−15
−16
−17
−18

0   1   2   3   4   5   6

Weeks

Start date (write yours in):

139

Weight Loss Chart

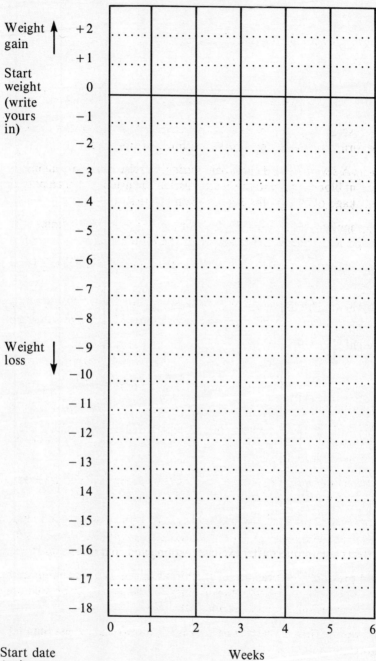

Weight gain ↑

Start weight (write yours in)

Weight loss ↓

+2
+1
0
−1
−2
−3
−4
−5
−6
−7
−8
−9
−10
−11
−12
−13
14
−15
−16
−17
−18

0   1   2   3   4   5   6

Weeks

Start date (write yours in):

Glossary

Aneurysm A weakness of a blood vessel wall. This sometimes suddenly forms a bubble and breaks, with catastrophic results.

Angina A severe central chest pain during exercise caused by an insufficient blood supply to the heart muscle. The usual cause is a partial blockage of one of the heart's main arteries.

Anticoagulant A tablet of warfarin or similar drug which 'thins' the blood and reduces the tendency of the blood to clot.

Aorta The biggest artery in the body. This carries blood away from the left ventricle and supplies the whole body.

Arrhythmia This is an abnormal rhythm of the heart. This may be because the heart is beating too fast or too slowly, or else is beating irregularly.

Artery A main blood vessel that carries blood away from the heart.

Atheroma This is a deposition of fatty matter in the wall of the artery.

Atrial fibrillation Abnormal disorganised contractions of the muscle fibres of the upper chambers of the heart preventing the more efficient simultaneous contractions of all fibres. This is often not too serious a state of affairs.

Atrium These are the two upper chambers (right and left) of the heart. These act as 'turbochargers' for the ventricles beneath.

Beta-blocker This is a drug which has many effects, including reducing heart rate, blood pressure and incidence of angina. Possible side effects are tiredness after exercise, asthma and cold fingers and toes.

Blood pressure The pressure of the blood (given as a maximum and minimum value) within the arteries. It is usually expressed in millimetres of mercury (eg 140/80).

Bradycardia This is a heart rate that is too slow (usually less than 60 beats per minute).

Capillaries. These are the smallest blood vessels in the body and occur in every tissue.

Cardiac Of the heart.

Cardiac arrest A life-threatening condition when the heart stops beating. The muscle may still be contracting in a disorganised way (fibrillating) but no effective pumping occurs. If the heart is not re-started within four minutes permanent brain damage occurs.

Cardiovascular Of the heart and vessels, usually arteries.

Catheterisation An investigation to find the blood pressure within the different chambers of the heart. It determines the efficiency of the valves and presence or absence of holes in the heart.

Cerebrovascular accident A stroke.

Cholesterol A blood fat, especially present in meat obtained from mammals (red meat).

Co-arctation of the aorta A narrowing of the aorta present at birth.

Collateral circulation When there is a blockage in a main vessel, a small parallel vessel increases in size to carry the main vessel's blood.

Congenital defect An anatomical defect occurring from birth. Serious ones are rapidly fatal. Less serious ones cause problems later in life.

Coronary arteries These are arteries that supply the heart. There are two (right and left). A heart attack occurs when one or both become blocked.

Coronary care unit (CCU) A specialised unit for looking after heart attack patients. When admitted to such a unit patients usually have continuously recorded ECG to monitor the state of their heart. They can then be resuscitated quickly in the event of a sudden problem.

Coronary bypass graft An operation in which a vein is taken from the leg of the patient and used to bypass a narrowing of the coronary artery.

Cyanosis A blue colouration, especially of the lips, caused by a lack of oxygen in the blood.

Defibrillator An electrical device that is used to restore normal rhythm to the heart. It is used when the heart muscle is beating in a disorganised fashion (fibrillating).

Diabetes (mellitus) A disease caused by a partial or complete lack of the hormone insulin. This deficiency gives rise to raised levels of blood sugar and sugar in the urine.

Diastolic pressure The minimum blood pressure that occurs within arteries in the body.

Digitalis A heart drug with many actions. It can improve the heart's efficiency.

Diuretic A 'water tablet'. It acts on the kidneys in order to increase the production of urine. This then has a secondary effect on blood pressure, and also reduces the load on the heart.

Drip A method of getting rapid control of the blood pressure and circulation by inserting a needle into a vein in the arm. Extra fluids and drugs may be given through this method.

Echocardiogram A three dimensional reading of the heart muscle, obtained by using very high frequency sound (ultrasound) as radar.

Electrocardiogram (ECG) An essential test for any diagnosis of heart disease. The minute electrical impulses running within the heart are measured and recorded via wires attached to the chest and limbs.

Embolus A blood clot that starts at one point in the circulation, eg calf or heart valve, and goes to another, eg lung or brain respectively.

Endocarditis An infection of the heart valve.

Exercise ECG An electrocardiogram carried out whilst the patient is running on a treadmill or else cycling on a static bicycle.

Fibrillation Disorganised contractions of the heart muscle.

Haemorrhage Bleeding.

Heart attack A sudden interruption of the blood supply to the heart muscle, caused by a blockage of a coronary artery.

Heart failure A partial failure of the heart as a pump to circulate blood around the body and/or the lungs. Frequent signs of this problem are ankle swelling and shortness of breath.

Heart/Lung machine An essential machine for many heart operations. It takes over the function of both the heart and lungs whilst one or other of these is being operated upon.

Heart murmur An extra sound in the chest due to some abnormal flow of blood through a heart valve. It may be heard by stethoscope.

Hypertension Raised blood pressure.

Hypoxia Lack of oxygen in the blood.

Ischaemic heart disease A broad term covering both angina and heart attacks. Both are due to lack of blood flowing through the arteries supplying the heart muscle.

Lipid A type of blood fat.

Myocardial infarction A heart attack, caused by the heart muscle being starved of sufficient blood.

Myocardium Heart muscle.

Oedema Excess swelling, often in the legs, frequently caused by heart failure.

Pacemaker An electrical device, often put inside the chest, to make the heart beat regularly.

Pericardium Membranes surrounding the heart.

Platelets Tiny cells in the blood which are responsible for clotting.

Pulmonary Relating to the lungs.

Rheumatic fever A disease now relatively rare which may occur in childhood. Later in life it may cause problems with the heart valves.

Risk factor A factor which may be associated with an increased likelihood of suffering a disease.

Saturated fat Animal fat which is usually solid at room temperature.

Sphygmomanometer The device used to measure blood pressure.

Systolic pressure The maximum blood pressure that occurs within arteries in the body.

Tachycardia A pulse rate that is faster than would be expected, eg greater than 100 beats a minute at rest for adults.

Thrombosis A blood clot that occurs in a blood vessel.

Unsaturated fat Vegetable fat which is usually liquid at room temperature.

Vascular Of the blood vessels.

Vein A vessel carrying blood back to the heart.

Ventricle One of the lower chambers of the heart.

Ventricular fibrillation A very serious condition caused by the disorganised contractions of the muscles of the ventricles. If not rapidly treated this causes unconsciousness and death.

Useful Addresses

Addresses and phone numbers given below are correct at time of going to press. If you require information, don't forget to send a large stamped self-addressed envelope.

A & A Marketing Media and Publishing Consultants
20 Coppice Walk
Cheswick Green
Solihull
W Midlands B90 4HY
Tel: 05646 2186

To obtain a copy of the *Heart and Stroke Screening Passport* please send 60p plus a large SAE.

Accept Alcoholism Clinic Counselling
200 Seagrove Road
London SW6 1RQ
Tel: 01-381 3155

Publishes information leaflets and offers advice on alcoholism.

Action on Smoking and Health (ASH)
5-11 Mortimer Street
London W1N 7RH
Tel: 01-637 9843

Publishes information leaflets and advice about stopping smoking.

Al-Anon
61 Gt Dover Street
London SE1 4YF
Tel: 01-403 0888

An organisation to advise the relatives and friends of alcoholics.

TCH—J

Alcohol Concern
305 Grays Inn Road
London WC1X 8QF
Tel: 01-833 3471

An advice and information service for alcoholics.

Alcoholics Anonymous
Consult local telephone directory

Publishes leaflets, advises alcoholics and offers group therapy sessions.

Anticipatory Care Team
Radcliffe Infirmary
Woodstock Road
Oxford OX2 6HE
Tel: 0865 249891

An organisation for members of the Primary Care Team interested in promoting preventive care.

British Diabetic Association
10 Queen Anne Street
London W1M 0BD
Tel: 01-323 1531

Publishes leaflets and advises patients on diabetes.

British Dietetic Association
103 Daimler House
Paradise Circus Queensway
Birmingham B1 2BJ
Tel: 021-643 5483

A professional organisation for dieticians. They keep a list of approved dieticians.

British Heart Foundation
102 Gloucester Place
London W1H 4DH
Tel: 01-935 0185

Publishes information leaflets on prevention and treatment of heart disorders.

British Nutrition Foundation
15 Belgrave Square
London SW1X 8PS
Tel: 01-235 4904

Publishes leaflets and offers advice on diet.

British Red Cross Society
9 Grosvenor Crescent
London SW1X 7EJ
Tel: 01-235 5454

Publishes First Aid Handbook and runs training courses for first aiders.

British Wheel of Yoga
1 Hamilton Place
Boston Road
Sleaford
Lincs NG34 7EF
Tel: 0529 306851

Publishes list of approved yoga teachers and courses.

Chest, Heart and Stroke Association
Tavistock House North
Tavistock Square
London WC1H 9JE
Tel: 01-387 3012

65 North Castle Street
Edinburgh EH2 3LT
Tel: 031-225 6963

Publishes leaflets and offers advice for patients and relatives.

Citizens' Advice Bureaux
Consult local telephone directory

Offers advice on a wide range of legal and social problems.

Coronary Prevention Group
60 Gt Ormond Street
London WC1N 3HR
Tel: 01-833 3687

Publishes leaflets and offers advice on coronary prevention. Please send
stamped self-addressed envelope with 60p stamp for information.

Family Heart Association
PO Box 116
Kidlington
Oxford OX5 1DT
Tel: 08675 79125

Publishes leaflets and advises about inherited tendencies to develop high
blood fats.

Health Education Authority
Hamilton House
Mabledon Place
London WC1H 9TX
Tel: 01-631 0930

Publishes leaflets on many subjects, ie heart disease, diet, exercise, stopping smoking.

Heart Beat Wales
PO Box 2010
Cardiff
Tel: 0222 378855

Publishes leaflets and offers advice about avoiding heart disease.

Medic-Alert Foundation
11-13 Clifton Terrace
London N4 3JP
Tel: 01-263 8596

The Oxford Prevention of Heart Attack
**   & Stroke Project**
The Oxford Centre for Prevention in Primary Care
Radcliffe Infirmary
Woodstock Road
Oxford OX2 6HE

Contact Ms Elaine Fullard on 0865 249891, Ext 4300.

St John's Ambulance Association
1 Grosvenor Crescent
London SW1X 7EF
Tel: 01-235 5231

Publishes First Aid Hand Book and leaflets, and runs courses to train
first aiders.

Samaritans
See local telephone directory.

Offers telephone advice and face-to-face counselling to desperate and suicidal patients.

Scottish Sports Council
Caledonia House
South Gyle
Edinburgh EH12 9DQ
Tel: 031-317 7200

Publishes lists of sports centres and courses.

Slimming Magazine Club
9 Kendrick Mews
London SW7 3HG
Tel: 01-225 1711

Publishes a list of commercial slimming clubs.

Sports Council for Wales
National Sports Centre
Sophia Gardens
Cardiff CF1 9SW
Tel: 0222 397571

Publishes lists of sports centres and courses.

Transcendental Meditation
Roydon Hall
Seven Mile Lane
East Peckham
Near Tonbridge
Kent
Tel: 0622 813243

Publishes lists of courses and approved meditation teachers.

Further Reading

Chobanian, Aram V., *Boston University Medical Center's Heart Risk Book: A Practical Guide for Preventing Heart Disease*, Bantam 1982.

Goodliffe, Colin, *How to Avoid Heart Disease*, Blandford 1986.

Grant, Ellen, *The Bitter Pill*, Corgi Books 1986.

Jackson, Gordon, *The Healthy Heart*, Salamander 1986.

Joseph, Simon, *Knowing About Heart Disease*, W. Foulsham & Co. Ltd. 1985.

Lloyd, Eileen, *Heart Disease and Your Lifestyle* (Prevention Health Guides), Rodale 1982.

Niazi, Dr S.K., *The Omega Connection: The Facts About Fish Oils and Human Health*, Esquire Publications. (Available in the UK from Northcote House Publishers Ltd.)

Further Reading

Index